I turned back to the desert. It was bigger than ever, and lonesomer.

DESERT WIFE

BY HILDA FAUNCE

INTRODUCTION BY
FRANK WATERS

WITH ILLUSTRATIONS BY
W. LANGDON KIHN

UNIVERSITY OF NEBRASKA PRESS
LINCOLN AND LONDON

Copyright 1928, 1934 by Little, Brown, and Company, renewed
1961 by Hilda Faunce Wetherill
Introduction copyright © 1981 by the University of Nebraska
Press
ALL RIGHTS RESERVED
MANUFACTURED IN THE UNITED STATES OF AMERICA

First Bison Book printing: 1981
Most recent printing indicated by the first digit below:
7   8   9   10

Library of Congress Cataloging in Publication Data

Wetherill, Hilda Faunce, 1890–
    Desert wife.

    Reprint of the ed. published by Little, Brown, Boston.
    1. Wetherill, Hilda Faunce, 1890–   2. Frontier and pio-
neer   life—Arizona.   3. Navaho   Indians.   4. Pioneers—
Arizona—Biography.   5. Arizona—Biography.   I. Title.
F811.W48   1981   979.105   80–22163
ISBN 0–8032–1957–1
ISBN 0–8032–6853–X (pbk.)

Reprinted by arrangement with Ruth Jocelyn Wattles

∞

CONTENTS

ILLUSTRATIONS

ACKNOWLEDGMENT

While living on the Navajo Reservation, I wrote a series of letters, a sort of running commentary of my experiences, to my cousin, Ruth Wattles. Those letters form the kernel of what has now grown into the book, "Desert Wife."

Among Miss Wattles' earliest memories are those of Navajos sitting about the big fireplace in the ranch home of her parents, waiting to be fed. She grew up with a lasting respect and friendliness for the Navajos, and in her high-school days was engaged in collecting their legends. Graduate work at the University of California, where Miss Wattles took her Master's degree, gave her an opportunity to read volumes of material on these Indians, and without her guidance and literary aid, "Desert Wife" never would have come into being. For this collaborative effort she should receive full credit.

HILDA FAUNCE

INTRODUCTION
by
Frank Waters

This is the compelling narrative of the wife of an Indian trader in the desert wilderness of the Navajos
before World War I. No other book about life at such
trading posts equals its revealing portrayal of the land
and the people, and its implication of the racial differ-
ences still confronting us today.

My opinion is grounded on a firm bias.

When I was a boy in Colorado Springs, my teacher in
Columbia grade school was a perceptive young woman
named Ruth Jocelyn Wattles. Ours was an unruly class.
Instead of punishing us for misbehavior, she rewarded
us if we were quiet by reading stories at the end of the
day. Our favorites were stories of the Navajos; and
most of these were excerpts read from letters written
to her by her cousin, Hilda Faunce, from the remote
trading post of Covered Water in Arizona. Miss Wattles's own familiarity with navajos who had come to her
home ranch in Mancos, Colorado, embroidered the
stories. But it was the letters themselves that held us.
What wonderful tales of a strange people in a far-off
desert land!

INTRODUCTION

They all came true a few years later when my two old-maid aunts took me to live for a time at the also isolated trading post of Shallow Water in New Mexico. Here were the same immensity of sand and sage, the same tribesmen riding in on horseback or in old springless wagons to trade and squat motionless for hours in front of the post.

Miss Wattles meanwhile had sent excerpts from her cousin's letters to *Harper's* magazine. Published there, they aroused the enthusiasm of Little, Brown, and Company, who persuaded her and Hilda Faunce to arrange them in book form. The book was published and reprinted in 1934, and now is being wisely reissued in its present format by the University of Nebraska Press.

The terms of its appeal to us now are magnified by the perspective cast by the years and changes that have happened since—changes that have outwardly transformed the land and "The People," but have not altered the enduring realities that still imbue them.

Hilda Faunce's narrative begins when she and her husband, Ken, are living in Oregon. The perpetual rain and fog are depressing. The bank fails. Hilda can endure these discomforts and reverses. Her husband can't. He was desert-bred, had once been an Indian trader in the Southwest. He is homesick, has to go back.

So they pack their belongings in a light spring wagon and drive back to Ken's desert heartland. There are few fences, roads, and automobiles. Camping at infrequent waterholes, they finally reach the Four Corners country where four states touch: Arizona, New Mexico, Utah, and Colorado. Ken is home. He buys the abandoned trading post of Covered Water near Black Mountain. It is 20 miles from the post at Chinle, Arizona, their nearest neighbor; 105 miles from Gallup, New Mexico, the nearest town.

The trading post is a decrepit two-room shack of rough planking held together by box boards. The back door opens into a storage tent for goat hides, sheep pelts, sacks of wool, supplies. Nearby, the seepage from a spring fills a well covered with boards: "Covered Water."

There is not a tree in sight. All around, interminably, spreads the vast empty plain. Into the post seeps sand, snow, loneliness. Without privacy, Hilda huddles in the back room peeking through the blanket hung over the doorway. She glimpses the Navajos spitting on the floor, picking lice from their hair, begging coffee. Their dark faces are strange, their customs queer, their language she doesn't understand. Ken feels perfectly at home. He speaks Navajo, builds up his trade, sending hides, pelts, and huge sacks of wool by six-horse teams to Gallup.

Gradually Hilda learns to speak Navajo, makes friends with Old Lady, Slender Girl, Hosteen Blue Goat. Helping Ken in the store, she learns to estimate the amount of sand cheating Indians put in their sacks of wool. They begin to prosper, saving money to buy someday a little farm of their own. Yet over all Hilda senses the old antipathy between the red and white races, the strange place-spirit so inimical to an alien newcomer.

She succumbs to a serious illness that affects her mentally and physically. She can't eat. Her hair falls out. She "seemed to be turning into an Indian," becoming "a deep, burnt orange color all over." If she died, the post would be a total loss. No Navajo would ever step inside it. They might burn it; that was their way. They have stolen the shovel; Ken would be unable to dig her grave outside. There is no escape, even in death. So Hilda worries in moments of lucid consciousness.

A doctor in Gallup is sent for. He stays twenty minutes and charges $225. It is not too much for the 105-mile drive. He leaves Hilda some pink pills and advises an operation in Gallup if she lives.

Hilda lives and undergoes a gall bladder operation. A month later Ken meets her and drives her back to Covered Water. This is the psychological turning point in her life. En-Tso's herb tonic restores her hair. And from now on she accepts without question the different ways and beliefs of the Navajos, even when they kill one of their members for having robbed a grave of jewelry. "Why do we try to thrust our civilization on a people like this?" she asks herself.

Without prejudice or sentimentality she recounts their hard and courageous life. A cyclone kills two little boys with their sheep. An epidemic of influenza leaves dead bodies in their hogans, which are then burned over them. Smallpox wipes out family after family. Hilda rides to others to immunize them with vaccine. When World War I breaks out, every Navajo man is ordered to register for the draft at Fort Defiance. Talk spreads that they will be put in front and shot first to save the white men. The Navajos, resolving never to leave their homes and their land, make plans to burn all trading posts and to kill every white man on the reservation. Ken averts the possible massacre. . . . Incident after incident that must be read in her own words. And finally after four years, having saved a stake toward their small farm, Hilda and Ken leave Covered Water.

A timeless book that needs no postscript to bring it up to date. Yet it may not be amiss, perhaps, to add that a short time ago I met Miss Wattles again after more than a half-century. When she opened the door I exclaimed, "Miss Wattles, you haven't changed a bit!" To which she replied pertly, "You haven't either, Frank, except that you're now wearing long pants!"

The Navajos are no longer a seminomadic people following their flocks of sheep. They have increased to a population of 150,000, becoming the largest Indian tribe in the United States. Their immense 25,000-square-mile reservation is the largest. It is also the richest, with vast deposits of coal, oil, uranium, and other resources. Industrial development of them is devastating great expanses of land and causing serious pollution of the air and water. Yet the comparatively small tribal income from it is providing roads, modern housing, school and health-care facilities. This "nation within a nation" is governed by an elected chairman and seventy-four members of the tribal council. Demanding the right to manage their own affairs, they are often in political conflict with exploiting private interests and the bureaucratic departments of the federal and state governments. But despite these long pants of their own that they are wearing, they are still the people with the integrity, courage, and beauty which Hilda Faunce portrays in this enduring book.

DESERT WIFE

I · OFF HIS RANGE

KEN closed his book with a snap and turned toward the window, where street lights served only to reveal the gray fog, layer upon layer folded about the house.

"What a hell of a country," he said. "We'll go back to my old stamping ground; I've had enough of this."

Ken was a desert-bred man, and the fogs and rains of the Oregon coast were attacking his joints with rheumatism; he hated so to get wet the rain was to him a personal affront.

I put more wood in the heater; it was hard to keep out the damp.

The weeks of doubt had ended in a bank failure which we feared would leave us with scarcely enough to

3

pay our bills. The house would have to go; the part interest in other enterprises we had worked so hard to pay for was gone.

It was late when we went to bed; the eaves were pouring a stream; the fog seemed to condense and flood everything. I listened to the boom and roar of the surf coming faintly across the sand hills and to the nearer moan of the foghorn at the old lighthouse and the sirens of the boats on the bay. I loved it all; every drop of rain, the soft water, every enveloping fog, all the lush green things that grew so over night.

With the coming of morning Ken went to his work as usual. So soon after the bank failure there could be only uncertainty, and why discuss uncertainty?

He left the house without speaking, but, having been married to Ken for seven years, I had learned something of his silence and could wait.

If our loss should include all we had, we could, as Ken had said, return to his old stamping ground, the great Southwest. I knew he was homesick. Weeks before I had been digging about in an old trunk and had come upon a white buckskin shirt, a relic of Ken's Indian trading days. It was made of four beautifully soft, white-tanned skins; it was sewed with sinew and the natural edges of the skins were fringed; the deer tails still dangled from the neck flap. An old medicine man had given the shirt to Ken.

Ken picked it up from the bed where I threw it. He held it for a moment at arm's length and then, pulling it over his head, he walked through the house and stood gazing out of the front window. The rain was falling steadily. Across the street some people who had collie dogs for sale had turned four of them out to romp and play. I could hear them barking and spattering through the puddles, as I leaned over the trunk again. In the very bottom, rolled in my own faded brown riding skirt of corduroy, was a pair of silver inlaid spurs. I carried them to Ken and, hearing the jingle, he turned and took them in his hands and then stared harder than ever out of the window.

These things carried him back to the days when as a young man he had been a trader on the Navajo Indian Reservation in New Mexico and Arizona. This had been years before I had known Ken — but it was his stories of those years that had first aroused my youthful interest in a man almost old enough to be my father.

Our dog, Tige, a white pit-bull, every neck bristle on end, growled to himself as he looked at those other dogs. Tige didn't like collies anyway.

We had had ninety-seven inches of rain that year. This was bad enough; but it was not this only that made Ken, accustomed as he was to desert country, feel, as he expressed it, "off his range." He had never known the hour-timed day, the on-the-minute appointment. Used only to solitude, he was silent to a fault and made few friends. His stern and desert-seamed face, with the lids squinted over gray-green eyes that were used to looking great distances in the dancing heat or down a gun barrel, did not draw people to him.

The friends I made did not come back after they had met him a few times; perhaps they sensed a desire on his part to be left alone. I knew he felt, somehow, that all man's ownership of the earth was gone, where there were so many to claim it.

A week passed, with what we could call ours lessening day by day. One noon Ken bought and brought home a team of horses. Because the previous owner had not been able to care for them in town, he had sent them to be pastured in a field where there was no shelter. Standing for weeks in the rain, both horses had contracted mud fever, an "Oregon disease", Ken called it. An ugly and painful skin affection it was. Ken at once secured a barn where the horses could be kept dry and through the days that followed he suffered with them; he could almost feel the mud fever breaking out on himself, and we counted the days until the sores on the animals would heal and the hair grow in again.

While we tended them, we learned to love them. Full brothers they were, bright sorrels of Steeldust stock. Early training had shown they were not quite fast enough for the track so they had been broken to saddle and harness for town use. Teddy and DeWitte were their names, and we called them Teddy-Witte for short.

While the horses grew sleek and glossy in the barn, allowed out only on the few and short periods when it was not raining, Ken went daily to work that bent his shoulders and deepened the uncertain look in his eyes. It was not only our own money and property he was trying to save; others had invested; and, while Ken was in no way responsible for their original investment or the management of their funds, he did his best for them as for himself. I packed a barrel of dishes and a box of household goods to be stored. Bit by bit, we gave away the furniture until the house was bare and empty and echoed to our footsteps. I tried to forget it had been home, the only home we had owned in our seven years together.

When the sores on the horses were healed, Ken led them away one morning to return with them hitched to a light road wagon.

A good horse was to Ken a pal and a brother. If he had lived sixty or more years earlier, he would have been in the foremost wagon of the first wagon train of the Forty-niners. Even in 1914 he always traveled with a team and wagon — the hardest way and the most earthy to move one's habitation or to see new country.

The day came when we were selecting clothes and cooking utensils for the trip. We had talked little, but I had been sure from the first that we would return to Ken's old "stamping ground"; at least, we would turn toward the Southwest and go until we found work, — work that meant food and clothes and a new start.

All morning Tige played in the yard; at noon he was dead. A neighbor had sent in a salmon caught in the waters of the bay and we did not know that the blood of a salmon was deadly poison to dogs. So few people know anything about love of dogs, I was ashamed for my friends to know how terrible the loss was to me. With Ken so silent and always unmoved, I was dependent on Tige's response to any interest and enthusiasm of mine. Life looked flat indeed, and I could not speak or breathe when I thought of going back to the sunshine and leaving him there in the rain. I wrapped him in a woolen skirt of mine and buried him beside a white rose bush in the yard where he and I had romped together.

Our camp load weighed in all less than five hundred pounds. There were our suit cases, a grub box, a bed roll, a bale of hay and a sack of oats. The desert water bag of canvas and a ten-gallon water keg seemed superfluous in the steady downpour of rain, but we had them.

With something like tolerance for Ken's vagaries and pity for me, the neighbors came to see us drive away.

As we reached the edge of town, Ken stopped the team and passed me the lines. He got down from the wagon and went into a house. As he never explained any act, great or small, I sat in the rain and waited. Soon he returned, carrying under his coat a little puppy. Dogs always liked Ken, and he was sheltering this one from the rain as she nestled in the bend of his elbow, happy and contented. He put her in my arms.

He had said nothing when Tige died. Perhaps, subconsciously almost, he realized that his habitual silence, though I often understood it, left me isolated and sometimes lonely. Now the gift of the puppy gave me the old certainty of his feeling for me, though it was not in his nature to put it in words.

Ken looked straight ahead; but, hugging the puppy in my arms, I turned and looked back at the little Oregon town that had been home for five years. Trouble with the one man Ken had counted on as a friend had made him want to get as far as possible from the cattle country of Colorado. After a cross-country trip with two wagons and two bronco teams, I driving one of them, we had stopped on the Oregon Coast. I had been willing to go anywhere, anyhow — with Ken — and I still was. Even before we turned the corner that hid the Oregon town from my sight, I looked at Ken. His eyes were on the road ahead, and I too looked straight to the front.

II · FOLLOWING THE OLD
OREGON TRAIL

THE fenced highway between fields became a road flanked by uncut timber and vines, often thick and high as a wall — the rank growth of a rainy country in rainy season. The horses splashed and tugged at the wagon which slithered from side to side in the mud or dropped into holes to the hubs. For the mud we often substituted corduroy, not bottomless but rough. In one such section we saw, some two feet below the line of travel, scraps of newspaper and mail-order catalogues. We were interested enough in roads to look closely to satisfy ourselves that this strip had once been worse and that some harassed mail carrier had sacrificed his second-class mail to make a mudhole passable.

Wet camps — two of them — as we climbed the coast

range, drew no comment from Ken, but I knew he must be thinking of desert country and its sun. Lady Betty, as we called the puppy (she was an English bull terrier) slept on my side of the bed, which was next to the wagon. We stopped at farmhouses before we camped to get milk for her, which I put in a cup securely wedged between the curve of the wagon wheel and the ground. When the puppy cried for food in the night, I pushed her toward the cup. She would creep back to bed, whimpering a little, but with her little sides distended with milk. Always after, she insisted that her food be placed next the wagon wheel and could scarcely be persuaded to eat from a dish placed elsewhere; when she was thirsty, she ran to the wagon wheel.

Early morning starts. Breaking camp at sunrise, the first traveler of the day sees the web of night in a million silver strands stretched from the tallest tree to the ground. Fairy telephone wires beaded with dew they are. Driving through them breaks the tiny threads with the whispering sound of old silk being torn. In this way we broke road to the top of the Coast Range and down the eastern slope. Once, for miles ahead of us, we could see the dainty, pointed footprints of a deer.

It no longer rained; the road was dry and through the long days the sun shone. We crossed the Oregon-Idaho line and began to make our nightly camps by water holes — water holes where Forty-niners had halted their wagon trains, for we were following the Old Oregon Trail.

We could always trace the area of black, tramped ground where the wagons had formed a square with the live stock in the center; around the water hole the earth was even darker and richer, where the oxen had stood drinking. The half of a rusted and pitted ox shoe that I found in such a place seemed historic and somehow pitiful.

In such spots I felt the ghosts of men, women, children, oxen, scattered fires, noise and movement. Then the sun dropped from sight beyond a horizon of sagebrush-covered hills. The quick western night with its clear stars and howl of a coyote followed. Ken called and I turned back to where, holding a frying pan, he crouched over a handful of fire. We were alone in what seemed an unpeopled world.

Other Travelers

One night we had nearly finished our meal when we heard the sound of a wagon and horses' shod feet on the hard dirt road. A brake squeaked and a man spoke to a team. Another camper had stopped for the night at the old camp ground. Our little fire made us visible, and in a few minutes we were hailed and a man stepped into our circle of light.

Whiskers! The first thing I saw was that he wore whiskers, whiskers that could have come from St. Louis in the early days. His blue overalls were faded, patched and stuffed into heavy boots. He wore a blue flannel shirt with big white pearl buttons and a slouch hat.

Ken remarked on the weather. The stranger commented on the road. They agreed that water was scarce and that the horses suffered less on a cool day when they did not get so thirsty. I feared the man would go before we learned anything about him, and he did turn to me and say his woman would be wondering why he did not come back. Woman — I couldn't keep still any longer. "Will you take some of our fire over to start your camp?" I said. "And won't you bring your wife to see us when you have finished supper?"

The man looked at me; then, doubtfully, at Ken. "Sure we will. My woman will be right pleased to see you and thanks for the fire."

He stooped and grasped the unburned end of a stick and, holding it so the blaze would keep alive, he returned to his own wagon. We could see the two forms moving about a small fire. They were not sixty feet from us, but we were separated by the darkness.

Ken cautioned me not to ask questions or talk too much. That rather dampened my ardor, because I did want the strangers to talk about old days. Ken never asked a personal question in his life nor ever answered one.

Before the visitors arrived, I dragged the bed roll close to the fire and spread Navajo blankets and sheep pelts. When they stepped into our firelight what I had hoped was true: she wore a sunbonnet, a wool dress, a checked blue gingham apron with a ten-inch band of cross-stitch above the hem. Down the front of her much-darned, snug-fitting waist were close-set, steel-cut buttons. She took off the sunbonnet and smoothed the already smooth gray hair with her lined brown hands. Her face was brown too, and lined. She sighed and smiled and I tried to think of the right thing to say without asking questions.

The men were discussing the road. The woman leaned towards me, as we sat on the bed roll, and said softly, "How long you folks been on the road? Where are you going, when did you start and where did you start from? I know it's none of my business and Jim told me not to ask; but I'm curious, that's all."

We hitched along the bed roll and put our heads together. One of the men said something about a horse with a sore shoulder. After that, we heard them no more. She talked and talked and stopped for breath while I talked. Where we came from, where we were born, where we were going, how we liked to cook and what our husbands would and wouldn't eat, how many children we had. She took my hand and patted it, when she learned I was childless. She told me how much canned fruit, preserves, jelly and pickles she had put up earlier in the season; she gave me her best recipe for pickled peaches.

She said she liked to sew and I said I'd rather crochet. She wished we could be together long enough so she could teach me to knit — I should be working on my man's winter socks right now; she was. Right then she took a half-knitted sock out of her apron pocket and, stopping only for a breath between needles, she worked as fast as she talked.

They lived six days' drive to the north; their family was grown — the last girl married and living in Salt Lake City. And now, in a lowered voice, came the news: they were on their way to the temple to be sealed. Thirty-five years they had been married, but what with the ranch and babies taking all the time, they had never been able to go to the temple. In the thirty-five years neither husband nor wife had taken any kind of a trip for business or pleasure. Now they would be sealed and be together in heaven, forever and ever. Had my man and I been sealed?

Ken heard that last question, as the strangers rose to go. When they were well on their way, stumbling through the darkness to their own camp, he said, "I told you so. I told you not to talk too much."

I was too breathlessly surprised at being taken for a Mormon to answer back.

Danger!

Climbing the long swells from horizon to horizon, the Old Trail ruts stretched toward Great Salt Lake and we followed them. Because our outfit was lighter than that of our fellow campers, we outdistanced them at once and did not see them again. For four days we crept through the wide valleys of sagebrush with the heated air shimmering above it, four days so nearly alike that scarcely a landmark changed enough to tell us that we had moved at all. The rolling swells of sage heaped higher and higher to what seemed to be a final crest that would surely break and change the monotony; but when we reached that crest, there was another succession of gray waves to climb. Horizons forever moved back, leaving us, as in a dream, following the broad ribbon of trail through the middle of an endless bowl of dull gray earth, but unable to get anywhere.

Even the horses felt the uselessness of haste. Usually Teddy-Witte showed great interest in what might be around a curve in the road or over the top of a hill and hurried with pricked up ears to get the first view; now they were dull and uninterested, because nothing changed. Though they went willingly, I could see that they were bored with Idaho, just as I was myself.

The turning wheels, the clink and squeak of trace and neckyoke, the grit of shod feet in the road were the only sounds. Ken squinted off into space; there seemed to be nothing else to do and I squinted too. Occasionally the wind brought a dust cloud down the road to envelop us and pass on; I imagined such were from phantom wagon trains passing; in reality, there was nothing moving in the whole universe but ourselves and we could not get anywhere. My eyes centered on another dust cloud, smaller than the last but coming down the trail as usual. I sighed at the hopelessness of getting sufficient water for a bath and waited for another stratum of dust to be deposited; there were several already and taking a bath in a cup of water was the best I could look forward to.

The dust cloud moved slowly, but it was not until Ken remarked that some one approached that I could believe that another living thing would really be out in such a world. Since this was the only moving object beside ourselves that we had seen for four days, I was interested. It was an hour before we met, but at last we were close enough to distinguish one man on the seat of a light camp rig not unlike our own.

Both teams turned out and slowed almost to a standstill; the men nodded a greeting; both spoke sharply to their teams and the horses jerked into a brisk walk again. I knew the horses wanted to stop to visit, but the men didn't.

We went without a word for a mile or two, then I said, "Where do you suppose he was going?"

"Somewhere back there, where we've just been," Ken answered.

"Do you suppose he knows, or is he just going, the way we are?" I guessed again.

"He knows where he is and he's not going very far this trip."

"How do you know that?" I asked.

"Because his horses were shod only in front," replied Ken, and did not speak for another mile. Then, "His dog is trying hard to overtake him. Look down the road."

I did. We both watched the animal. At first it was barely a speck on a rise of gray road in the distance; then it became clearly a dog, coming toward us at a lope. Teddy-Witte, stepping more quickly, threw up their heads and watched; Teddy snorted and pranced, and as I look back, I know Witte showed uneasiness.

For several moments we could not see the dog; but the next rise in the road would bring him closer and the next still closer. Ken and I were staring hard at the top of the slope just ahead, where he would surely come into sight any moment, and the horses were becoming restless and uneasy. Suddenly the animal loped over the crest. On the instant we all knew that something was very wrong. Before I could speak, Teddy-Witte lunged and the wagon was bumping and swaying through the brush. Ken had turned the horses off the road and into the sage.

"Coyote," he said, "and mad. Get the rifle quick." The beast, while Ken spoke, fell down, rolling and gasping in a convulsion. Unable to move, I had not left my seat, when he staggered to his feet and came plunging forward along the road again.

"The rifle, quick."

I swung over the back of the seat into the wagon box and started frantically to find the gun. It was under everything. I dragged wildly, hopelessly it seemed, at the bed roll, at the sack of grain, and finally had to move the grub box before I got the rifle out and free of the leather scabbard. Thanks to Ken's habit of keeping a gun always loaded, I didn't have to dig for the cartridges.

When I could hear, Ken was saying, "Quick, put it in my hand. I don't want to lose sight of him."

His hands were reaching out and I put the gun into them as I climbed back to the seat; he never looked down but let go of the reins as I took hold of them. The horses would not stand still. "Hold them quiet; I've got to shoot from the wagon," Ken said.

I set the brake hard and allowed my eyes to turn toward the road, where the coyote was now almost parallel with us. His head low and swinging from side to side, he was coughing and whining weakly. I was too frightened to move. The horses continued stepping uneasily and snorting. I quickly rolled the puppy, head and all, in a sweater and put her between my feet in the bottom of the wagon box. I feared for the horses' legs if the brute should turn from the road — how I wanted to get Teddy-Witte off the ground and safe from those wet, snapping jaws!

The coyote staggered across the road directly toward us, but when he struck the bushy sagebrush he snapped at the stiff branches that touched him and turned again down the road. Ken was looking down the gun barrel. I held my breath and whispered to Teddy-Witte to hold perfectly still, but they moved uneasily until it seemed as if shooting and hitting would be utterly impossible. Ken was sitting sidewise in the wagon seat, his feet crossed under him tailor fashion, his back to me. He always sat down to shoot a rifle and stood up to shoot a shotgun or throw rocks — all equally deadly, it seemed to me, in Ken's hands. Then the roar came. The horses lunged, the wagon jerked over the tough branches of the sagebrush.

"Is he dead? Is he dead?" I kept saying, though I couldn't take my eyes from the horses to look. Ken took the lines and turned into the trail; the horses were snorting and wanted to run.

"He's dead, all right; but we'll have to go and drag him out of the road."

The coyote lay motionless, the froth wet around his jaws and spattered over his heavy ruff. Taking hold of the bushy tail, Ken dragged the carcass to one side and we left it there.

As we drove on our way, Ken turned to me almost triumphantly. "You had the idea that nothing interesting could happen in this country. Now, you see."

We did not get to water that night but made dry

camp with what water we had in the kegs and a sage-brush fire.

We made our bed on the ground as usual. That seemed to me a risky thing to do, but Ken made no change in our normal procedure except to place the rifle where he could reach it from the bed.

The horses would not sleep or even stand quietly but stood twitching their ears and staring into the night. Witte kept throwing his head up, as if to smell every breeze, and Teddy jerked at his rope and pawed. Twice he dug his forefeet into a hole and I got up and moved him. Each time I stood by him a minute and we both listened until my ears hurt. The gasping whimper of a mad coyote would not carry far, even on a still night. If Ken spoke to the horses, they reached out towards the bed and heaved an exasperated sigh but did not quiet for more than a minute.

About two o'clock the moon rose. Ken looked at his watch and began putting on his clothes; I was only too glad to do the same. He put the load into the wagon, and I placed a box of cartridges on the seat and leaned the rifle, cleaned and loaded, against the bed roll, where it was within easy reach.

The horses were relieved to move and trotted briskly down the road. The night was like pearl: there was no breeze, no dust, no coyotes. The wagon seemed to make more noise than ever.

Daylight brought a new view at last; scrubby trees and rocks were in sight on a few high spots; and when we saw a fence and plowed land in the distance, we felt like shipwrecked sailors on a raft, sighting land after a storm; at least I did, and I stood up in the wagon to see if somewhere I could see a house. Ken saw it first though and had to point it out to me, a low dirt-colored thing of weathered boards. Near it was a haystack. We would stop and try to buy hay.

As we drove to the gate and pulled up, a man came from a pole corral where he was milking; another man carrying a pitchfork came from the haystack; they both looked us over quickly and, I thought, anxiously. Before they spoke, the door of the house opened and a woman hurried out. We all nodded and each waited for another to start. Something in the woman's face made me say, "Has anything awful happened here?"

"Have you brought bad news?" she half whispered, as she came to the wagon and put out her hand to take mine.

"No, only this. We killed a mad coyote yesterday; did he hurt some one?"

"You killed him? He's dead?" They all exclaimed and looked at each other with relief; then they all talked at once. It seemed that the mad coyote had been there and had bitten a calf and two chickens and had then got away into the brush; and since they had been unable to follow him, they could only kill the bitten calf and the chickens. A man had ridden to warn the next neighbors, who were fifteen miles away, but he had not returned. They would have to carry guns to the fields with them for the rest of the season. As this was the third mad coyote, there must be more. The situation made every move dangerous and every day a risk to themselves and their stock. They were more than appreciative that we, strangers going through the country, should have taken the time to stop and kill, rather than avoid the mad brute. We bought some hay for our next night's camp and drove on.

Almost immediately we were back in a world made up exclusively of sagebrush flats, with here and there a knoll covered with scrub piñon, where the low swishing of the wind in the stiff branches was the only sound for miles upon endless miles, and that is the sound that makes one more lonesome than anything else on earth except the howl of a coyote. We saw perhaps a dozen lizards in a day and they were an event.

Once I surprised myself by asking Ken if he were lonely. We were almost asleep and I had the feeling that in the whole world there were only ourselves and the stars. Ken surprised me by answering, "No, I'm not lonely. Every coyote that howls, every locust that rasps tells me, 'I'm glad you're back'." That was a long speech for Ken, long enough to keep me awake for an hour, thinking.

One day, far on the trail ahead of us, we saw a moving speck. Of course, I thought at once of mad coyotes, but this moved too slowly. An hour later a heavy team and wagon drew alongside and stopped. Since it is road etiquette for the lighter team and wagon to give at least half of the road — all, if possible — we turned out. The man looked at us and I at him. He had two barrels of water in the back of the wagon. Over each was a piece of sacking held in place by a barrel hoop.

"How far is it to water?" Ken asked. The stranger turned and pointed back the way he had come.

"Six miles beyant you come to the Old-Timer's Place. There's a spring there, but it's only a water hole this time of year. Some fellow tried to build a home there. You'll camp there to-night. Reckon the stock will have the hole tromped full of sand. It's that way every week when I go down."

He stopped talking and gave his full attention to looking us over.

"Where do you haul this water?" I asked, because I knew Ken never would.

"Well, you see, I've taken up a homestead out here about twenty miles and haven't had time nor money to dig for water yet, so I'm hauling from the Old-Timer's spring. I've got a hundred acres in wheat and it sure looks good. It burned out last year and year before, but it looks good now. You can't beat this country for soil and climate."

Ken was interested now. In both drivers' hands the lines hung slack; the teams nodded in the sun. A locust droned and for an hour the men talked and I listened. The soil, the seasons, the rainfall, the market, and again the wonderful soil.

"I hadn't never used my homestead right," the stranger said, "and now that the family is growed up and gone, the wife and I thought we'd prove up on a six hundred and twenty-acre desert claim."

"Is it lonesome?" I asked.

"What say?" He scratched a bony forefinger through his beard. He had to think that question out. "Not so's you'd say lonesome," he concluded. "The nearest neighbor's only thirty miles beyant; and if the wheat makes good this year, more settlers will come in."

Both men looked out across the endless sagebrush and said it was a fine country. I looked too. It was all gray sage, as high as a horse's back, and in some places the stems were four inches through. Such a growth could thrive only on good land, but there was no water; and the country was desolate and forsaken to the last faint cry of lonesomeness.

Again the men talked and I listened with an apprehension that was physical. It was such a country as this Ken knew and he did not know what it meant to be lonesome; if ever any one needed to find work, we did. I had reason to fear we had reached the end of our trail.

At last we did drive on, came to the spring, and rocked it up so we could dip a pail in. We filled the smallest keg and got supper. Near the spring a part of the foundation of a house still stood. To one side was a small yard for flowers or a child. I wondered which. A woman had helped to build the house, rock up the spring, clear land. I wondered how long she lived here and if another woman had ever been in her house.

Ken left his camp fire and went again to look at the spring. He remarked that he had never used his homestead right. A cold chill swept over me and that evening I neither sang nor talked and he asked if I were sick. The next morning there was not water enough to fill our big keg, and Ken shook his head, hitched up the teams and we followed the Old Trail flowing ahead of us over the hills. Somewhere beyond the pale blue of horizon was Salt Lake. The horses trotted; the rings on the tugs and the singletrees jangled; wheels gritted as they turned.

Salt Lake City

At last, quite suddenly, we came to a ditch running brimful of water. Ken got out the bucket and gave each horse a drink, and then just stood there and looked at the water. It was muddy; but there was so much of it, it seemed perfectly beautiful.

We were nearing the Great Salt Lake. From the old, old trail we looked out over a green valley. On our left was the snow-crested Wasatch Range, all steep and shadowy. On our right were the outlying pools of the lake which alternated with patches of salt crust. Far out they blended into one and flattened into the distance that was Western Utah.

From the Old Trail we drove into good roads between good wire fences, with irrigating ditches full to the brim running alongside. There were orchards and fields, houses and people. We drove through Ogden by the back streets, for Teddy-Witte were more upset by automobiles than by anything else in the world, and their weeks in the country had made them even more skittish when they got into town. Given plenty of room, they would bow their necks and, snorting and prancing, circle around an automobile; but in close quarters they were truthfully full of fear and panic and had one idea — to turn around, regardless of space, and go in the opposite direction as quickly as possible.

In earlier days the horses had been crashed into by

a car that came upon them in a closely wooded lane, where they could not turn out. There had been a quick right-about, a runaway and a general smash-up, and the lasting memory of that sprang into instant and awful terror at sight of an automobile. Now I wondered how we would ever get through Salt Lake City.

By keeping to the outer edge of the highway, we covered the distance from Ogden to the larger city as calmly as possible. To me the city meant the first and only touch with friends left in the coast country. We were to call for the first mail since our journey began. Mail! For endless weeks there had been no word from friends. Now we would locate the post office and perhaps there would be some word of affairs left behind. We had even a bit of hope that one piece of property might still be ours; we had not waited for the final reckoning.

Trying to pick the most quiet streets, we entered Salt Lake City and at a corner store obtained careful directions for reaching the post office.

In my own mind I was wondering how I would ever be able to hold the team while Ken went in after the mail. One thing I was sure of was that I could never be persuaded to go for the mail myself. My poor camp clothes made that decision final. I had not felt embarrassed along the Old Trail and not much in the small towns, but this was altogether different. I was ashamed to appear on a city street in the faded and shabby garments that seemed unimportant in camp, and there was no time or place to change; so I would stay in the wagon and Ken's corduroys and flannel shirt could go for the mail; but, I wondered, could I hold Teddy-Witte from doing something terrible while Ken was gone? How long would it take him to get our mail from a city post office where he might have to stand in a waiting line?

The smooth pavements made the wagon roll so easily that the horses could give all their time to prancing; they ducked and twisted every time a car passed and took up all the space on their side of the street, even including the sidewalk. We were too busy watching them to see what attention we must have attracted, though it passed through my mind that those who did notice us would think we were on the way to the temple to be sealed.

The automobiles were thicker than ever, both parked and moving, and Teddy-Witte were in a steaming panic of fear and had a most pressing urge to run away from all that noise and confusion. We turned another corner and met a street car broadside, just as an auto whisked around us and under Teddy's nose, almost touching him. He was already on his hind legs and as he turned to come down, his forefeet struck the step of the moving street car and almost threw him. There was a wild scramble of people and cars, trying to give us room, and room was the one thing we all wanted most of anything. Snorting, and groaning on the bits, for Ken was standing braced and leaning back on the lines, the horses leaped forward. I was holding hard to the wagon seat with one hand, but held the other ready to grab Ken's belt and hold him, if they should jerk him overboard. The sound of the eight feet on that echoing pavement was like a drum corps.

From the corner of my eye I could see staring, astonished faces. The wheels struck the street-car track, the
wagon flew up, came down, struck another track,
bounced again, and again. It was terrible. It seemed as
if we must have somehow got into a freight yard —
there seemed to be so many tracks to cross.

Some one shouted in an angry voice, one that the
horses didn't like, "Hey! Stop! Stop! What you trying
to do here, anyway, young feller? You walk your horses
across those tracks, d' y' hear!" A policeman appeared;
and, since every one else had halted, Ken managed to
stop the horses and the officer came up to the wagon. He
looked from Ken to the horses and back to me. I know
I looked anxious, but the idea of any one ordering us
to go slow, when it was the one thing we would have
liked to do, was so funny I laughed.

Ken explained to the officer that we wanted to get
out of the city the shortest way, but that we had to stop
at the post office first. The blue uniform pointed to
a building ahead of us and nearer than we hoped.
"Right," he said, "there's the post office and this street
will take you out of town. Just keep on going before
that team of broncos does real damage around here,"
and waved us away. The traffic all started at once and
my heart came back up into my throat and stayed there.
We stopped in front of the post office and Ken passed
the lines to me.

"Hold them still," he ordered and got out; he went
to the horses' heads, rubbed them, and stood with
them for a moment. Teddy-Witte immediately relaxed,
sighed, nosed Ken and did not seem to see a car that

stopped right in front of them. Ken turned and went up the steps and disappeared into the post office. I sat there, the reins slack, the horses resting, the cars whizzing by. Minutes passed, the horses were getting nervous, beginning to fidget and throw their heads; both started to dig a hole right through the pavement.

"It's a pretty wild team you've got there." I looked up to see the policeman standing beside the wagon. He stayed there until Ken came back and then directed us out of town again.

No news from affairs we had left, no word of hope that any small part of the wreck might be salvaged; but there was a friendly letter from the neighbors who missed us. All the little coast community seemed so far away that it was an effort to remember that I once had a neighbor; our entire little world moved down the road, foot-loose and unattached.

III · FROM SALT LAKE TO
NEW MEXICO

Hoping to reach open country, we waited until
the day was almost done before we began to look for
a place to camp; then, for the first time since leaving
the bay, we had to ask a farmer for permission to camp
on his land.

We stopped near a barn where we could see a man
dashing about, apparently trying to do his chores in
record time. Very evidently impatient, he paused between jumps to talk to Ken. When Ken waved to me
to come, I drove up beside the man in time to hear
Ken say, "I'll be with you in a minute to help with that
wire."

The farmer hurried around the corner of the barn
and Ken explained, "He's covering his hog pens with

chicken wire and wants to finish before dark. I'll help him."

I was left to make camp and did so leisurely, as one glance told me the pens were not small. The hammer blows and the excitement in the farmer's voice told me the men were hurrying. When the work continued after dark, I lighted the lantern and went to hold it so they could see to work.

The farmer was not so excited now; but I could see that he was very tired and his face in the lantern light was streaked with sweat.

It seemed that late in the afternoon he had learned that his neighbor had cholera among his pigs. Both this farmer's pigeons and his neighbor's flew back and forth from hog pen to hog pen. The chicken wire was to prevent the pigeons flying from the cholera-infested pens and lighting among these pigs where there was no cholera.

Ken and I returned to camp in time for a ten o'clock supper and bed, but I could not sleep. Our contact with this man, hurried by the necessities of living, was too much of a contrast with our life on the Old Trail.

At daylight the next morning Ken and the farmer, each carrying a shotgun, were doing chores. When a flock of pigeons fluttered to the barn roof, the four barrels roared at once. We were invited to stay for pigeon-pie dinner but refused and drove on. The last we saw of the farmer he was telephoning for freight cars to get his fat porkers to market.

A Rock as a Weapon

The long days flowed on, followed by a new camp each night — a new camp that was hard, stony, rough, steep and, as the season advanced, cold. Traveling rather later than usual one afternoon, we completed the climb up a divide that must have added four hundred feet to the altitude. We were looking for water and could see signs of it as we approached the summit. The road, overshadowed by cliffs and bordered by huge bowlders, which in the ages had rolled from the cliffs, found its way over the lowest point of the divide. The water, we discovered, was a ravine that led back two or three hundred yards from the road. We prepared camp speedily, as the ravine brought the hour of darkness closer.

The horses, glad enough to reach a spring and the green grass around it, seemed, I thought, a little uneasy; but Ken did not speak of it and I could not see that he examined our surroundings with unusual care.

We were finishing the camp supper when, echoing from the cliffs and with considerable distance adding unearthliness to it, a snarl brought me to my feet. Both horses stopped eating and threw up their heads, their nostrils and ears twitching.

Ken sat still. "Mountain lion," he said. "Not close."

I knew a mountain lion, unless very hungry or wounded, was a coward. "How do you know he's not close?" I asked.

"Look at the horses," Ken answered. "They're not

32

really scared and your own ears can tell you that fellow's a long way off."

It's queer that, while alertness never leaves a person sleeping in the open, a sense of security develops at the same time. The latter is probably due to the fact that the sleeper is seldom disturbed by anything really dangerous; and my sense of well-being was largely due to my acceptance of Ken's alertness, so I was quickly asleep when we crawled between our blankets, spread, as usual, on the ground. I had been asleep some hours when I was awakened by pain in my shoulder, where a stone had made a dent in the flesh. Rubbing the shoulder, I turned over and for a little while watched the moon rising white above the cliffs that looked inky black in the shadow. I was drifting off into sleep again when I realized Ken was whispering, "Get me a rock. Quiet. Reach me a rock."

I felt along my side of the bed where there had seemed to be nothing but rocks but now I could not put my hand on one. My stiff shoulder reminded me of the one under the bed. Gouging it out of the dirt with my fingers and feeling for Ken, whom I found sitting up in bed with his back toward me, I put it into his hand. For a minute he did not move and I knew he was staring intently at something. Perhaps he was waiting for the moon to rise a little higher.

Slowly, noiselessly, he began freeing his legs of the blankets. I held my breath for seconds. Suddenly, with one motion, he was on his feet and throwing the rock. The horses pulled back, dragging the wagon to which they were tied, and I jumped to hold them. In another

33

instant Ken had the rifle and the roar of it was deafening.

"Got him," he remarked.

"The lion?" I asked, thinking as I went to untangle the puppy from the blankets, where she was trying to bury herself, that the prowler could be nothing else.

"Yes," Ken answered. "He's been snooping around here for an hour, trying to get up nerve enough to steal the bacon."

"Did you get him with the rock or the gun?" I asked.

We took the flash light and investigated. The rock had broken the animal's shoulder but it was the shot that had been fatal. I did not expect to sleep after that, but I did. There's nothing so comforting as a dead lion.

For nights after that Ken took the gun to bed with him and I had a pile of rocks at my side; but we had no occasion to use either.

Mormons at Home

A lump comes into my throat when I remember the loneliness and hardship, fortitude and courage of these settlers of Utah. I shut my eyes and see the faces of the women we met. They were tired always, but determined, and had a look that made me think they were more isolated by something inside them than by geographical conditions.

Some living we saw that was not all hardship. At one more prosperous-looking ranch we stopped to buy feed for the horses and ask if we might camp for the night. As we drove up, a man in a near-by field was trying to move a hay derrick. The driver was nervous and excited and was yelling and sawing at a team more excited even than their driver. The horses would not pull together but lunged and plunged in a way to make the derrick rock dangerously.

Ken walked up to the outfit as if he belonged there; he took the lines and both horses and man quieted at once. Ken suggested that the man ride on the back of the derrick to balance it and direct where it was to be placed; the team settled down to steady pulling and in ten minutes the derrick was located and the men were shaking hands. Talking like old friends, they walked back to the wagon where I was waiting. Sure enough, Ken had discovered that the stranger was a brother of a neighbor of Ken's boyhood days in the Southwest country. Mr. B. insisted that we come in. He offered us a corral, a haystack, a pasture for our horses and took us to his home. The home, I saw, was two houses; two large white farmhouses, one green-trimmed and one yellow, faced each other across nice green lawns. Between them was a fence but connecting them was a well-worn path.

Our host took us into the nearer of the two houses, announced we would spend the night and introduced us to a pleasant, elderly woman; then he and Ken promptly disappeared. I had not spoken to a woman for weeks and it was delightful to meet one again; but my camp clothes and sunburn embarrassed me, and a feeling that Ken and I had all but asked ourselves to be this woman's guests did not make me more comfortable.

I think I looked the way I felt for Mrs. B. was more

than welcoming. Before she had made me feel entirely at ease, two little girls entered and very soon two more arrived from school. The children brought me their treasures to admire: a doll, a storybook, brother's new suit of clothes with the first long pants, a watch and chain from a mail-order house, an encyclopedia, the family album. They hung onto me and climbed into my lap, and how friendly and human they seemed. •

After an hour, the woman sent the children to wash for supper and took me to see work of which she was very proud. It was a cheese-making and curing house, where she did almost everything herself. As she showed the presses, vats and shelves full of really lovely cheeses, she explained that they lived so far from a railroad that it was necessary to concentrate their crops to make the marketing easier. The start of their fine dairy herd they had brought to this new country forty years ago.

At the supper table we were introduced to a younger woman, also Mrs. B., who was the mother of the four girls who had entertained me and of four boys. All eight were under sixteen years of age and were clean, well-dressed, healthy youngsters.

We sat down to a delicious supper of great slices of wonderful graham bread and a blue-and-white bowl of rich milk. There was nothing else except the blessing. This the father at the head of the table began, and it was added to by each, large and small, until it came back to the father and was finished by him at length.

After the meal, the children gathered around their mother, coaxing and whispering. I heard her say, "Well, do so then, if you think the lady is not tired of your talking and bother." Then to me she added, "They want to show you the baby's hair. We have to keep it in a net until she is old enough to take care of it herself."

I had noticed that the youngest child was as quaint as an old daguerreotype with her hair hanging halfway to her waist but confined in a silk net. Now she was led up to me and the net carefully removed. I had expected to see pretty curls but not such a glory of auburn and flame waves. Never have I seen hair like it; it was like the sunsets we would say were unnatural if we saw them painted. It would do no good to paint hair like that, for no one would believe it ever grew on a human head.

The whole family was as proud as could be of that hair but did not say so; they only kept repeating that soon Janet would be old enough to care for her hair herself and would not take others' time every day to put it in a net.

While I helped with the dishes, I was told that the older woman's family — twelve children in all — were grown and were all doing well as teachers, ranchers and stockmen.

We made rather a later start than usual from this interesting Mormon home. That night, or rather that afternoon, for we always camped about four o'clock, we were still in the irrigated section. To our right we could see a small town, a store and post office combined and three or four farmhouses. All the male population seemed to have turned out to corral a small black cow and her calf. The men were horseback and were using pitchforks, but the cow could not be driven in any direction; no matter which way they tried to urge her, she would lower her head and charge a horse with such ugly meaning that horse and rider retreated, or she would lower her head and stand pawing the ground like any mad bull. Finally the men gave up the struggle and left the cow and calf in the alfalfa field.

We learned at the tithing yard where we camped and bought feed that she had gored one horse that day. "Guess we'll have to kill her," one man remarked.

I felt sorry for the poor thing. Just some milk cow having a nervous breakdown over her new calf, it seemed to me. However, I could see the town's point of view. She had treed a dozen people, killed a horse and surely had earned the name of being really dangerous.

When we camped in the open, we made our bed on the ground and tied the horses to the wagon wheels, but near a settlement we made our bed in the wagon box. The night in the black cow's territory the horses were tied to the outside of the tithing-yard fence.

It was not yet daylight when I awoke and crept carefully out of bed, so as not to disturb Ken. I climbed out onto the wagon tongue, thence to the ground and felt my way along the pole to the end, where I had left the makings of the breakfast fire. Beside the fence the horses slept and sighed; they stirred and spoke softly to me as I squatted by the tiny blaze. Trying to see Teddy-Witte in the dim light, I raised my eyes, and there, on a level with my face, were two glowing balls of fire; the polished upward curve of horns caught the flicker of my little blaze. I could not judge how far they were from me but I knew they must be close, very close.

Not a muscle of me would stir. Should I get to my feet? Should I roll under the wagon? There was no time to do either and still I did not move. Seconds passed and a quiet, unexcited voice said, "Better get into the wagon." In one bound I was there — I never knew how I got to my feet or where I put them afterwards, but I picked myself up from the wagon bed as the cow hit the double-trees with a crash and rushed back into the darkness, where we heard her speaking softly to her calf.

I had not supposed Ken was awake. For some time after that daylight was an early enough rising time for me.

We were no longer on the Old Trail but were among the orchards and fields. Here was water and the green of summer foliage, glorified now and then by fall colors.

Five Years Ago

I looked forward to seeing the Green River ford. On our way to Oregon five years before, we had crossed the river in the same place. When Ken stopped the team before a concrete, steel-reinforced bridge and remarked, "This is it," I could not believe him. This clear stream could not be the torrent of freshet water, tumbling with dirty whitecaps. And where were the flat-bottomed scow and the wire cable of the old ferry? Ken pointed downstream. There was the scow on the bank, and there, still attached to the big tree, were the twisted coils of the cable.

The sun glinted on the water; a car slid across the bridge. I remembered that Fourth of July night five years ago, when we had stopped our teams and wagons on the farther side of the stream. The ferrymen, all of them drunk, were crossing only because the town with more whisky was on the other side. Until almost dark we worked, getting our two wagons and four horses on to the sloping, rocking boat. Once we were aboard, the wheels slid; the horses could not keep their feet; we all skidded and staggered as the boat butted blunt end into the swift current. The ferrymen were too drunk to pull on the cable effectively and we were too busy with the horses to help them.

Ken, quickly stripping the harness from one team, and shouting that it would give the horses a better chance to swim, motioned me to do the same for the other team. Working as fast as I could, I heard him shout above the noise of the water and the uproar on that scow, "If we go in, keep hold of a halter rope with one hand and a tail with the other. If you have to drop one, let go of the halter rope." I didn't know if Ken could swim; I knew I couldn't.

After an age, the boat scraped the bank; the men tied their craft to a loop of wire cable that was twisted around a tree and hurried off up the sandy road to town for more drinks. How good the solid ground felt! Thinking how much too much water there was in that river, we got the horses off the boat, hitched up and drove away.

Now, five years after that mad night, as Teddy-Witte trotted slowly across the bridge, I could count the stones in the clear, shallow stream below.

As we crossed another beautiful bridge over the Grand River at Moab, I had in mind that crossing also five years earlier. We had waited hours before attempting to ford a boiling torrent of freshet water. Bridges! How they do eliminate risks.

Colorado at Last

Out of Moab, Utah, we began to climb into canyons and out onto the high open ranges, not sage but the rolling mountain grasslands that Ken had been homesick for, back in the Oregon fogs.

The days were noticeably shorter and the nights decidedly frosty. We were often ten miles on our way by sunup. Cold! It was the end of the first week in October. One who has not got out of bed into all outdoors to break camp in that before-dawn darkness has no notion how cold and long are the two or three hours before day; neither has he any idea of the beauty of a new-born day, when the stars are frosty and the small hours so still that the only sound in the world is what you make just breathing. We halted early in the afternoon, as we needed daylight to make camp. Even the horses learned to pick out a good camp spot and often turned of their own accord into a sheltered nook or down a branch road leading to a stream.

Our food was simple. Canned goods were too heavy to haul and there were no gardens in the world of piñon breaks. Bacon, eggs, bread, apples, fresh meat as we killed it ourselves. Usually we had rabbit; once or twice there were doves or sage hen. Once when we shot a prairie dog to get oil for the guns, the meat looked so good I cooked some, but we had to throw it out. The animal was too old and fat.

We saw a few sheep which Ken disliked as only a cattleman could, but we saw no cattle. Even if both sheep and cattle had been thriving, how could we go into either business without money?

At Del Rio, a little mountain town in Southwestern Colorado, Ken was at home. Men greeted him by name and talked freely of business; but I saw him look at the rows of parked automobiles and I knew he did not want to stay.

An old friend of his, who lived on the edge of town, invited us to come to her house; but, because of illness in her family, she was worried and busy. We insisted on making camp as usual, though we were glad to be near her and have pasture and barn for Teddy-Witte.

By the camp fire that night Ken asked me to write a letter. Writing came awkwardly to him, as he habitually wrote even less than he talked. The letter asked a brother of his in Gallup, New Mexico, if he could tell us of a Navajo Indian trading post where Ken could get work.

We pulled the shoes off the horses, so they could rest better, and turned them into the alfalfa pasture; then we could only wait, until in early November the answer came.

42

New Mexico

A trading post was for sale, one hundred miles "in" from the railroad. Our chance, perhaps. Ken reshod the horses; we restocked the grub box, greased the wagon wheels, mended harness and patched the horse blankets; and then I shampooed my hair and we were ready to start.

November is no time for camping in high altitudes. Our first day's drive took us to a little New Mexico town Ken had known years before. At a ranch we were greeted by a real pioneer of the country, Kit Barton. It was heart-warming to see him hug Ken, hammer him on the back and call him "son." I was introduced and he was so cordial I wished he'd hug me too; but he didn't.

The men talked late that night of the old days, and the next morning Kit watched us ford the San Juan River, with the slush ice floating around the horses' legs. The half-dozen channels were all wide and swift but none more than breast deep to the horses; the quicksand, being half frozen, gave us no trouble.

Across that stream my spirits lifted. We were in Indian country — on the Navajo Reservation. Here was adventure! But on that first day we did not see an Indian nor any other living thing.

It was sundown when we drew up beside the store building of a trading post. It was low-walled, dirt-roofed and had small windows close to the eaves. There was a woodpile and an Indian dwelling or hogan.

Two men, surprised to see a woman, came out of the

store with Ken. They gave us all they had of comfort, but we made our bed under the frosty November stars and rose before daylight to continue our journey.

The next day we saw smoke from two or three hogans, but never did we see a hogan or an Indian. We passed petrified trees, the wood showing the color and grain so truly that I wanted to gather up an apron full of chips. There were mountains of sandstone like smooth, rounded loaves of bread, side by side in a pan; again there were cliffs and pinnacles, balanced rocks, windows worn by blowing sands of a million years. Then the mountains crowded back to make room for a gray expanse of menacing desert.

The horses stopped as if they realized that crossing that valley, matted as it was with dried Russian thistles, would be disheartening business. Ken examined the gray, prickly mass for the road we were following, but no rock or bend of it was visible, even to his eyes.

"We've got to cross it," he said, "and time means a lot to us right now, but we'd better eat before we start."

We gave the horses grain, a part of our last bale of hay, and a pail of water each from the keg in the wagon, and had a cold lunch ourselves.

As if they were plunging into a river, the horses breasted the thistles. The plants were all of two feet high and grew as thick as hair; no earth was visible. We took the shortest way across, but at the pace we moved there was a long half-day of hard work ahead. Teddy-Witte stopped every few yards to rest but were soon dripping wet; under every strap of the harness the sweat worked into white froth. We were two hours reaching the lowest part of the valley, where the spring rains had lasted longest and the thistles were the highest. They scratched the horses' bellies and Teddy-Witte twisted and lunged. They were tiring themselves needlessly but Ken could not quiet them. I could only hold on to the wagon seat with both hands and think the situation could not be worse.

In that I was mistaken. The dry growth began to accumulate in front of the wheels; the wagon acted as a hayrake to drag the stuff, which would pile up higher, higher and higher; at last the wagon would leave the ground, climb a windrow, balance on top, and then the front wheels would drop with a thud and we'd start the whole thing over again.

The sun goes down early in November. When it had set, the cold afternoon deepened quickly into colder twilight. I ceased to think but continued to hold on, because I was too numb and exhausted to change my position. It was nearly dark when Ken left the wagon and went to the horses' heads. He did not need to stop them.

He stroked them a moment and then began pulling at the thistle; he worked as if he intended to clear the way himself. I was too cold to wonder at him or to move to help. When he had made great heaps of the weeds, he touched a match to them. Cold as I was, I was a little amazed at that, for if one pile would burn, the whole valley might be swept by flames; but the thistle was not dry enough to burn without coaxing, and it took time to burn sufficient clearing for a camp.

We were too tired and cold to care for food; but we rubbed the horses down well, blanketed them, and put grain and hay before them. Then we spread our bed on the ground, and the warmth from the fire-heated earth soon reached us through the layers of sheep pelts and blankets which were our mattress. Warmth! Rest! Sleep! How heavenly! The horses discovered that the ground was warm and Teddy lay down and was soon snoring.

I had been a million miles deep in sleep when Witte's whistle brought Ken and me up standing. We were not ahead of Teddy, who was on his feet, snorting. Witte, his head high, was staring out into the night, and Ken leaped to cover his nostrils and prevent a repetition of that far-carrying whistle. When I saw Ken's action, I covered Teddy's nose. It was evident we should know the nature of the disturbance before we ourselves were discovered.

The moon had risen and was high and white in an inky black sky. The jagged sky line of hills was as clear and sharp as if cut from black paper. Standing in that zero air in our night clothes, we held our breath to listen; then let it out in a long, quivering sigh and held it again. At last we got the faint but unmistakable squeak of a saddle and the swishing noise of bodies moving through the thistle. In another moment we could hear the puff and snort of cattle being driven. The hills surrounding the valley were not quieter than we. The sound passed fifty yards from us, but we could see nothing until cattle and drivers climbed a little rise and were between us and the moon. We could not tell how many cattle there were, but driving them were three Navajos with blankets pulled over their heads as protection from the bitter cold.

We waited until all sound had died away and Teddy and Witte had become calm. It was Witte's turn to lie

down; Teddy stood, his ears twitching nervously, and we crept to bed, too frozen to comment.

The sunshine took away all the mystery of the night. Ken went to "read the tracks" and reported that three Indians had been driving five head of cattle. He added that they had probably stolen the cattle or they would not have been driving them at night.

It has puzzled me not a little to guess how Witte knew enough to give that whistle. He was a city-bred horse who had never had occasion to give a warning signal, yet he whistled like any wild stallion on lookout for the herd.

A Sick Horse

Two hours more "hay raking" and we were out of the thistle and on a rough, unworked road, but it seemed like a highway. The horses, glad to stretch their legs, swung into a bumping trot. It was near noon when we saw a windmill a mile or more to the side of our line of travel and, nearing it, we found a well-worn road leading to it. We were about to turn in that direction when we noticed a curving ditch bank. Evidently a ditch ran from the windmill. If there should be water in it, we would be saved the two miles to the windmill and back. I was just feeling thankful that of the many wells drilled on the reservation we had happened upon one that had struck water, when Witte stumbled and fell to his knees; he staggered a few steps and seemed to recover. We looked to see if he had stepped on a stone or if he had a loose shoe, but could see neither.

A few steps farther and with his feet spread wide apart, he began to sway and lower his head. We both leaped to the ground and I ran to his head, while Ken stripped off his harness. In a few seconds we had him clear of the wagon. He turned dizzily around a few times and fell.

We were within thirty feet of the ditch and there was a tiny life-saving trickle of water in it. Quickly Ken got out the shovel and built a little dam, so that in a short time we could dip up water with a tin can and fill a pail.

I had never seen a horse suffer with the colic. At

once Ken knew the cause. When we had last stocked up with provisions, we had had to buy some rolled barley instead of oats. Ken had fumed and scolded at the time, said any one ought to have sense enough to feed a horse oats. We had fed the rolled barley only once, as we still had some oats on hand.

Never before had I experienced the feeling of helplessness that came over me. Here we were, forty desert miles from the only appointment that offered shelter for the winter, a prospect of livelihood for the future.

In the grub box was a bottle of patent medicine — an old and pungent cure-all for man and beast. For five years we had carried that medicine and had carried also an empty bottle for administering it. Though I had little faith in the medicine, I was glad we had it. We mixed it according to directions on the bottle and gave poor Witte a dose of the awful stuff. If anything, he seemed to suffer even more.

There was no fuel in sight; and we had no horse feed, since we dared not risk giving Teddy more of the rolled barley. All we could do was to give him four apples. For ourselves we had cold canned peaches and a box of crackers, but with Witte suffering so we could not eat. We were thankful for the little stream of water; but even with it, the situation seemed hopelessly dark. The road we were on was so little traveled that no one would pass for days.

Knowing that a horse with the colic should be kept moving, we walked up and down with Witte. When he could walk no longer, he would throw himself down with a groan that almost broke our hearts. Then Teddy would come and hold his nose down to Witte's, and we could only stand back and wonder what Teddy would do in this world without his brother.

By four o'clock it was growing colder and would soon be dark. We felt sure Witte could not live until morning, and yet Ken did not have the courage to get the rifle and shoot him. The only thing to do, and that must be done without more delay, was to get another horse to help Teddy pull the wagon. We might yet keep our appointment; certainly we could not stay where we were. We recalled that some six miles back we had seen wagon tracks leading off the road. Out there somewhere there must be an Indian or Mexican dwelling.

We had no saddle with us; but we always used riding bridles with the harness, so Ken bridled Teddy and folded a Navajo blanket on his back to serve as a saddle. Before leaving, he led Teddy over to Witte and all three put their heads together. They were saying good-by; for Ken, at least, did not expect to see Witte alive again.

The next minute I was alone, in the fast-gathering dusk of that ghostly barren wilderness. Teddy's hoof beats grew fainter and fainter on the hard dirt trail. He was running, as Ken would have said, like a scared rabbit.

Witte, his head on the ground, got the vibrations of Teddy's feet. With what seemed like a final effort, he struggled in the most desperate way to get on his feet; he tried to whinny, then fell back. I ran to him and lifted his head, so he could look after his brother; he could see better in the twilight than I could.

He watched a moment and then began throwing himself about so violently that I put my shoulder to his and boosted every pound I could. Unsteadily he got to his feet and, with me leaning hard to steady him, we staggered down the road in the dark, each of us whimpering to the other.

I hope I shall never be called upon to live through another such two hours as followed. I could not keep poor Witte on his feet; there was nothing to do but let him fall. In spite of all my efforts he went down in the worst possible position, his head low in a rut. I tried to get him on his feet again, but he seemed to give up. I simply could not have Ken come back and find I had let the horse die with his head low; I ran to the wagon and got the ax and shovel. The edges of both were ruined when I finished, but I literally undermined that horse. I lowered his hind quarters until his body lay more comfortably than it had since he first became sick — and that seemed ages ago.

The moon came up with the friendly softness that makes one want to cry. It even interested Witte, and he lifted his head to look at the great, white ball as it rose from the black edge of the horizon high into the sky.

I became thoroughly warmed up and excited. Witte wasn't dead yet; maybe he would live, after all. The water in the little ditch was frozen and I had to keep moving to keep warm. I dug holes for Witte's forefeet so they would not slip from under him when I tried to get him up again; then I dug places for my own feet so I would not slip when I braced him.

Time after time I encouraged him and boosted. He

seemed to understand and would struggle for a little and then throw himself back with a groan that seemed to say, "It's no use. Let me die." At last I did get him to his feet; we staggered slowly back to the wagon and then both collapsed and lay still for a while with our heads together. If the coyotes heard me cry, I didn't care.

It was too cold to lie still long. Too tired to try to help Witte up again, I brought horse blankets and spread them over him. When he rolled in agony, I stood by and held the blankets; when he was quiet, I covered him.

I gave him another dose of the medicine, on sugar this time, and he took it willingly. I found myself talking to him as if he had been a person. I told him all about the situation; how he simply could not leave Teddy and Ken and me. We all had to have each other to live at all, and this was no time for one to go back on the others. When I stopped speaking, he raised his head; then I went and sat on the ground and we moaned together, Witte and I.

It was late and so still that I could hear the clink of the windmill two miles away, turning in the night breeze. Witte was better and sipped a little water. He lay still and did not seem to suffer so much. I was beginning to wonder how Ken would ever find us in all that waste, when we had no fire to guide him; I listened for his whistle out in the night. I listened so hard my ears hurt, and my blood seemed to stop in my veins because I willed it to.

At last a very small, high sound reached me. It came

twice before I placed it as the starting note of Teddy's high, shrill call. I ran to Witte, raised his head and told him to listen for Teddy.

He knew Teddy's name and pricked up his ears but did not seem to hear a sound. It was several minutes before I heard anything more myself, and I began to think I had only imagined that note, when Witte got it with the ear next the ground. With a quick whinny, he lifted his head and looked out into the night. I heard hoof beats at a great distance but coming nearer and nearer. Again Teddy's shrill call. It seemed so loud and near that I often wondered how far away he was when I heard that first high, birdlike note.

Of course, Ken supposed he was returning to a dead horse and an uneasy, sorrowing wife. Teddy only knew that he had to reach his brother in the shortest possible time. Never did running hoof beats sound so good to me. I could see only a short distance into the night; my ears told me that Teddy had been running a long time but was still going strong. I gathered up his blankets and stood waiting.

They were first seen only as vague dark objects; then suddenly Teddy leaped the little ditch and slid to a stop with his nose against Witte's. Ken dropped a sack of wild hay he was carrying and slid to the ground. Teddy was drenched and foaming. While I put on his blanket and buckled the straps carefully, those three had a real get-together. I staggered over to the bed roll and lay down.

I woke several times during the night. Ken did not come to bed at all but somehow got Witte to his feet and walked him up and down, up and down. Teddy stood at the wagon, eating the wild hay, but turning his head to watch every time Witte passed him.

In the morning, long after sunup, a Mexican arrived with a fresh horse, but here a new problem arose: Teddy was determined to kill the new horse. He bit and kicked until the Mexican exclaimed at our having such a vicious brute. Finally I held Teddy's head while the men hitched him beside the Mexican horse. Even Witte became excited and tried to crowd between the outsider and Teddy. Teddy-Witte both seemed to say, "If we were ourselves for two minutes, you could never put this over. We would do away with that animal entirely." They could not understand we were trying to help them; all they could see was that we were bringing a stranger into the family.

At last we were ready to start, Teddy fuming and Witte reduced to following. The Mexican horse proved to be a dead head and Teddy had all the load to pull. However, that did not prevent him taking time out to bite and kick. For a few steps he would give all his attention to pulling, and the strange horse would drop back until his doubletrees scraped the wheel. At that sound, the most maddening, to a nervous horse, Teddy would bare his teeth and, making a most savage face at the poor dumb stranger, he would try to take a piece out of him. Ken tried to urge the new horse to step up, but the sight of a whip completely demoralized Teddy. He acted positively demented.

Ken's patience was wearing thin and I was all worn out because Teddy-Witte loved each other so and could not understand that we were trying to help them. How little and how much animals can understand!

Finally, in trying to go ahead and kick at the same time, Teddy got a foot over the wagon tongue and threw himself. We stopped with a jerk. Ken took out the Mexican horse and put the harness on Witte. Instantly Teddy was calm. We adjusted the stay chains so Teddy would pull all the load and Witte would only help hold up the tongue. We went on, the Mexican accompanying us to help over the bad places by fastening a rope to the end of the tongue and to his saddle horn. Teddy tried to catch up with the Mexican horse even then and drive him away. Witte slowly improved. By noon we had covered five miles and were nearing a water hole.

At the water hole we found other campers, white men. Of course they gave us fire and over the coffee we told them of our predicament. Since we were keeping the same road as far as the night camp, the men insisted on taking our load that far, on dividing their hay with us, and on exchanging their oats for our rolled barley. Their horses, they said, were accustomed to the barley. The only way a person can repay that sort of kindness is to remember to pass it on.

Ken paid the Mexican and dismissed him. By night Witte was able and willing to eat his share of both oats and hay, and we could sleep in peace, listening to the horses contentedly chewing.

After a daylight breakfast we said good-by to our friends and turned to the little-used road that cut across to a mountain range that had been our western sky line for two days. Never was there such air, such sky, such roads. The horses stepped out briskly, their necks bowed and their chins tucked in. We were all so happy, just with health regained, that it was a wonderful day.

IV · A BUSINESS DEAL

ANOTHER twenty-four hours of slow travel to save Witte and we were in Gallup, New Mexico. In the early days of Indians, Mexicans and outlaws, it was the roughest, toughest town in the Southwest; now it was the distributing point for many Indian reservations. Here the traders, scattered over the hundreds of square miles of the Indian country, bought for their trade everything from velvet to soda pop; and to the wholesale houses from which they bought, the traders sent sheep, cattle, hides, wool, jewelry, Navajo blankets.

I looked eagerly up and down the dirty streets. There were automobiles, but there was also the clink of horses' shod feet, the jangle of spurs and the soft pad of moccasins.

I was glad and even Ken seemed cheerful.

We drove to Ken's brother's and on the steps met Mr. Taylor, the man who had a trading post to sell. He was looking for Ken. He knew of Ken's experience as a trader years before and the new deal was made so quickly I was breathless.

In an hour Mr. Taylor was on his way in a car to his own post at Lugontale. We waited two days to rest the horses and then set out on the sixty-five miles following him.

Such a life! Creeping across barren valleys and climbing rocky watersheds, we crossed the Continental Divide and were again on the Pacific Slope. Step by step we had covered the miles from Oregon to Gallup, had crossed the Divide as we went east and now we had turned, recrossed it and were in Arizona.

Each step seemed to carry us farther from every comfort, from the very last trace of civilization. More than once I was panicky. I wondered what Ken could see in country like this. The emptiness, the barrenness, the vastness threatened me. Almost I cried out to him to turn back; I could not face life in a country without one spear of green grass, with nothing but rocks and bare dirt, with never a human being in sight.

To keep from going mad in the stillness I counted to myself, keeping time to the horses' steps, or I gave myself a stiff neck gazing up into the deep blue sky to count eagles and buzzards.

Sometimes I could get Ken to play a sort of game, "I can see something that begins with the letter 'r'." The other looked carefully and named over every bit and part of horse and wagon that begins with r; then out across the landscape he gazed intently at nothing at all, but saw ranges, ridges, rocks, rainbows, and rabbits. It was just about as stimulating as playing solitaire, but it killed time.

I talked to the Lady Betty. I told her about prairie

dogs and rabbits and coyotes; about being a friend to Teddy-Witte and Ken and me, and how she should eschew the company of Indian dogs. She seemed as terrified of the country as I was and often climbed quivering into my lap. Again she would leap from the wagon and run around and in front of it, smelling of every stone and chasing every lizard until her foot pads were almost bleeding.

I sang all the old ballads, the Sunday-school hymns and coon songs. All I ever knew I sang, and "umpty-tummed" all I had forgotten.

In that vastness I could hardly hear myself and I began on verse. I said what I knew and hated myself that I hadn't learned more. One poem kept time better than the others with the rattle and jog of our progress. It went:

> There was a little animal, no bigger than a fox
> And on three toes he scampered over Tertiary rocks.

Suddenly I got to thinking that that animal, the little Eohippus, must have run over these very rocks we were looking at, and surely when the petrified trees we had seen were green, the anthropoid ape had lived in them.

Having found that the rhyme of the little Eohippus kept time to our movements, I could not forget it. It became irritating, then maddening. For miles on end I repeated that silly rhyme until it had no beginning and no end; still it kept time to the horses' steps; nothing in the world seemed to have beginning or end. I determined I would say nothing, nothing whatever;

I would be so much a part of the silence I would not suffer. Then Ken asked me why I was so quiet.

In desperation, I began on prose. I said what I knew of the Declaration of Independence and the Constitution. I even tried the multiplication table and cooking recipes.

And poor horses! Poor Teddy-Witte! One step at a time from Oregon to this God-forsaken waste. The Gobi Desert could not be more desolate. How would we ever get out? I looked at Ken. In his face was no anxiety, no uneasiness even. Once he pointed to a mountain fifty miles away on the sky line and said so and so happened beyond that.

I remembered. He had been here before. This was very truly his old stamping ground; it was not new and appalling to him. He was seeing familiar scenes, scenes like those where he had a trading post years ago, scenes unchanged by his fifteen years of absence. Unchanged? In my heart I knew that desert had not seen a change, except in sunsets, in ten thousand times ten thousand years.

The sunsets were never quite the same, but always they were the most awesome fields of color, that spread over the whole sky and shut down to the earth, enclosing the most terrifying loneliness of yellow rim rock, gray sand, red buttes, black streaks of volcanic ash, and water-washed clay hills.

Lost in it all were we five, little, live things, creeping along with three days' supply of food and water. Since our daylight start Ken and I had scarcely exchanged twenty sentences. Before dusk we camped by a water hole and made a tiny camp fire which after dark seemed at the very center of an uninhabited world made horizonless by starlight.

I had reached the point where I could have been made to believe that nothing existed in the world but Arizona desert, when we reached the end of the sixty-five miles and found there white men and women and children, Mexicans, Indians, ponies, dogs, the big house and enough shacks for retainers of the Middle Ages. There were freight teams arriving and leaving; there was noise, movement, talk.

Dinner with twenty white persons at the table, Indian girls serving, laughter and talk in Spanish and English contrasted unbelievably with a tiny fire in the desert with two human beings crouched beside it.

"We will try to make your wife comfortable here until the new building is up," Mr. Taylor leaned across the table to say to Ken. "No woman could live in that shack."

I looked at Ken. Part of the agreement was that Mr. Taylor was to erect a new store building; but after all these miles, was I to sit and wait?

In our own room later Ken said, "Maybe you'd better stay here a little while."

I nodded. What was there to say?

Ken Goes to Covered Water

When, a couple of days later, Ken went to hitch up, I automatically went along. The strange barns, the non-English voices and the smell of Indians had made Teddy-Witte wild. They were in a panic, and the men thought they were broncos and came to help Ken. He could have told them they were not needed, but I think he wanted me.

When a Mexican attempted to lead Teddy to the wagon, Teddy went up on his hind legs and ran snorting backwards. That started Witte and he kicked another Mexican and lunged for freedom. I started toward Witte, but a Mexican seized my arm and dragged me back. I would be killed, he chattered, if I went within arm's length of such brutes. Quite undisturbed, Ken was putting the last of the load on the wagon. He saw me rescued and gave me one look which bathed the whole mad scene in understanding and humor. Witte, snorting at the end of a taut rope, was daring the Mexican at the other end to do his worst. Hand over hand, I followed the rope to Witte's head. When I reached him, he nosed me softly, telling me his worries in little whinnies and breathings. I knew he was saying that if that fellow came near him, he would go all to pieces. I hitched him myself in his place beside Teddy, who also had a little tale to tell. Between them, they almost rubbed me off my feet.

The Indians and Mexicans looked on in amazement, and Ken said nothing. Teddy-Witte were so gentle and tractable when they were having their own way and such villains when they were excited or wanted to show off.

Mr. Wolfer, a helper who was to go with Ken, threw a suit case and a bed roll into the wagon and climbed to the seat beside Ken. "You'll not ask me to do anything with this team," he said. "I don't know horses and I don't want to know 'em, sir."

A BUSINESS DEAL

Lady Betty, aquiver with eagerness, looked from me to the wagon. A running jump to the seat landed her in the stranger's lap. Uncomprehending, she leaped back to the ground and ran round and round in circles. She leaped up to lick Teddy-Witte's noses and then ran to me and off again, around the wagon.

"All set," Ken called, and the horses sprang forward with their necks bowed and their mouths open. Lady Betty yelped, ran around the moving wagon and back to me. "Go with Ken," I told her. "Go with Ken." Instead, with a bound she threw herself into me amidships, and I held her for a moment. When I put her down, barking at every jump, she flew after the team that was already splashing through the shallow waters of the Pueblo Colorado, the arroyo on which Lugontale is built.

Such a parting! I laughed to myself, even while there was a very real ache inside me and my eyes blurred so I could not see the team out of sight. We had come so far together that any parting seemed tragic.

Weeks later, Ken told me of his trip. An Indian never cares if he has a road or not and he drives a team as he rides a pony — across country. No two Indians ever want to go from the same place to the same place; and a wagon track in that almost rainless country may be visible for months, so a flat valley is crisscrossed with meaningless roads.

Because Ken had never been in this section of the reservation before, Mr. Wolfer was to guide the outfit to the Black Mountains and the tiny spot that we were to know as Covered Water; but they no sooner reached one of those valleys of crisscrossing roads than Wolfer was completely lost. Of course, Ken had received directions — the kind of directions that mean something to a "desert rat" and to him only. In this case, he had a range of red hills to go by, or around, or over; but he had hardly come in sight of them when a rare desert fog settled down close and he could see no landmark of any sort. Trusting to his instinct for direction and location, he went as straight as might be through that maze of hills and buttes and purposeless trails to the shack that was Covered Water store.

Lugontale

When Ken, Teddy-Witte and Lady Betty were out of sight, the Mexicans and Indians who had watched the hitching up went back to work and I returned to the "Big House", a house with five-foot-thick adobe walls, with a beamed ceiling of two-foot logs and a living room thirty by eighty feet. Between the ceiling logs Indian baskets of value were nailed to the ceiling; the walls were entirely covered with etchings of Indian heads, family portraits and every possible Southwestern scene done in oils. A couch seemed misplaced until I realized that lying there on one's back gave the ideal view of the baskets on the ceiling. The floor was covered with Indian blankets. A fireplace in the center of one side of the room accommodated three logs that were carried in one at a time, a man at each end. My room opened off the opposite side of the big living room and before daylight each morning I heard the men come in, speaking softly in Spanish as they carried out the ashes and made up the fire.

A BUSINESS DEAL

Of all the treasures in the room, I shall longest remember the saddle pockets or panniers of bull's hide with brass locks and hinges. My host told me these had been used by his grandfather to pack "pieces of eight", the gold doubloons of the good old pirate days. Now they held only the dust cloths used by the Navajo maids.

Every one at Lugontale had a job and looked after it. I tried to help. Often I could only watch the bread brown in the outdoor ovens, where two hundred loaves a day were baked for the family and hangers-on and for sale in the store. It was in the kitchen that I first saw Mexican chili made and realized that it was one of the most delicious, satisfying and most frequently counterfeited dishes in the world. The making of that was not left entirely to servants; one of the ladies of the house did the work or carefully supervised it. No New England mincemeat ever received more devoted care or ever so thoroughly justified the pains taken with it.

Mr. Taylor had half a dozen Fords which were in use when the roads were passable; however, when the roads disappeared in sand or mud, teams and wagons became the means of conveyance. I soon learned that the garage and repair shop were not the least busy places and that the freight storage depot was far from being the least interesting place at Lugontale. Daily I was fascinated watching the Mexican and Navajo teamsters drive out into the horizon with loads of case goods, flour, tin cups, saddles, or come crawling out of the distance or over a hill with hides, gay blankets, wool, orange and black pottery. Out there, where these came from, was a new life I was to know.

DESERT WIFE

I Go to Covered Water

In two weeks I had not become really acquainted with all the busy life at Lugontale; but when Mr. Taylor announced one morning at breakfast that he would go out by auto to see how Ken was getting along, I was delighted to go. We started at four in the afternoon, in a Ford touring car with a new driver. I learned afterwards that there was generally a new driver. Mr. Taylor always slept when riding in a car, so he wanted to go day and night. Naturally, after a trip of a few days or two weeks, there was a new driver. On this occasion we were scarcely out of sight of Lugontale when Mr. Taylor went to sleep; but Mrs. Gray, his daughter, and I enjoyed the ride. To me, after thirteen hundred miles in a camp wagon behind a team, the speed seemed miraculous.

At first we dodged among low, piñon-covered hills to come out suddenly into a big valley. Here the main road led southwest into the Hopi country, where the pottery was made. Our road — two shallow trails running parallel over bunch grass and cactus — led west. Distant square-cornered or flat-topped ranges with white or red fluted sides, bright in the lowering sun, were pointed out to me. A blue-black range, the only one having an irregular sky line, I was told was Black Mountain. It tapered off to a flat point in the north but piled — rough, jagged and black — against the blaze of the sunset in the west. Our trading post was located a mile to the left of a certain sharp peak.

Suddenly we slowed down. The engine sneezed and

stopped. Mr. Taylor awoke. The driver climbed out and looked in and under. We were stuck. Charlie went to work with tools spread out on both running boards; Mrs. Gray and I scrambled through deep sand to the top of a little hill; Mr. Taylor trudged away toward a bluff and was out of sight almost instantly.

Suddenly the sun was gone. The east was a glory unbelievable until one looked at the west. Here was a jumble of blue and purple cloud shadows and scarlet flame high lights with gigantic rays of brilliant yellow shooting high into the heavens. There was color in the desert itself,—not in vegetation, but in the very earth and rocks. In the afternoon sun the reds and blacks and blues had seemed unreal enough; but I would never have believed, had I not seen them, what they could be in the light of the sunset.

When only a faint purple was left above the jagged sky line of Black Mountain, Charlie gathered up his tools. "No use trying to work now," he said. "I can't see and we haven't a flash light." Almost before he finished speaking, it was dark and we three were alone. The country that had looked like a dried out fairyland was now nothing but shadows and black spots. To our right was a miniature canyon, perhaps fifteen feet deep, that had attracted our attention because of the alternate layers of pink and yellow sandstone composing its walls. Now we scarcely dared move, lest we stumble into it. Well we knew we could not scale those smooth walls.

Mr. Taylor had been gone quite two hours and now his daughter was convinced that, bewildered by the coming darkness and his near-sightedness, he had fallen into that canyon or another. Charlie, the driver, started to hunt him; but Mrs. Gray, panicky now, held him. We could not have him drop out of sight too.

I could not believe that anything had happened to even a near-sighted man who had spent sixty years in this country, but his daughter was genuinely alarmed. At last, promising to keep up a continuous whistling or shouting, Charlie left us to hunt Mr. Taylor. His whistle was still piercingly near when he turned back toward the car where we two women sat wrapped in the lap robes.

"I told you the old man was all right," he said, as if he had not been anxious at all. "He's coming now with an Indian and a lantern. There's a hogan near by where we can at least have a fire."

We did not dare leave anything loose in the car for Indians to steal, so we gathered together tools, chains, blankets, canteen, shovel and had ourselves well loaded by the time Mr. Taylor and the Indian arrived.

We started. The lantern, almost hidden in the Indian's flapping blanket, gave us only an occasional faint gleam of light. I never knew there could be so many rocks in one desert; and as we stumbled and staggered, I began to wonder why we had not gone back to Lugontale or built a fire by the car.

The old gentleman kept up a continual puffing and scolding. He scolded because the car broke down, then because Charlie did not get it fixed before dark, then because he might not be able to get it fixed to-morrow and we would have to get horses to pull us out. He had already sent an Indian to fetch the horses.

A BUSINESS DEAL

After what seemed miles and hours, we came to a square building, not a hogan. Light from a fireplace in a corner showed through an open doorway. An Indian woman disappeared through another doorway as we entered. Apparently we were being given possession.

The firelight showed a small adobe-walled room. Along two walls, making a right angle, was a high counter of packing-case boards with lettering on them, — Arbuckle's coffee, Del Monte peaches, showing clear and black. The shelves behind the counter were empty. Beside the fireplace was a pile of wood and near it on the floor were a quarter of raw mutton, a coffeepot and four cups.

There was no furniture whatever, so we spread the blankets on the floor and sat on them. For both warmth and light the fire was an improvement on the lantern, which we extinguished to save oil. The house, Mr. Taylor told us, had been built by an Indian school man for a store. He had failed as a storekeeper, as all such men do, because of the unbreakable custom among the Navajos that as long as a man has anything he feeds his relatives.

In a little while coffee was boiling and meat broiling on a bed of coals dragged out of the fireplace onto the dirt floor. There was no salt, no sugar or cream, but the meal was satisfying.

As soon as we had eaten, Mr. Taylor took off his shoes, stretched his feet to the fire and was snoring in ten minutes. The ground was as hard as a cement sidewalk, and, besides, the rest of us were younger and not accustomed to sleeping under such conditions. We whispered and giggled.

We napped at last. It must have been nearly morning when there was a peculiar snuffling sound behind the counter. I sat up, listening. The fire was almost out and the room was very dim. Nevertheless, in two minutes I was sure that Indians were sleeping on the floor behind the counter. How absolutely quiet they had been! And how cold they must have been, too, shut off from the fire! Every one else was asleep, but I could not doze again, and lay wishing for Lady Betty to warm my back.

All at once it was daylight and while we were eating more saltless mutton and drinking black coffee, we were suddenly in an immense world of sand and sunshine.

By the time we reached the car — the distance was but a few yards by daylight — an Indian was there with a harnessed team. Half a dozen other Indians were there too.

The team was hitched to a rope fastened around the front axle. The driver of the horses climbed up astride the hood of the car, and the other Indians, directed by Mr. Taylor in fluent and continuous Navajo, got down from their ponies and pushed. Of course we were seated in the car, so it took a lot of pushing. Those ponies would not stir a step until the car was shoved against their heels; then they leaped forward with a jerk; the driver alternately flapped the lines and sawed on the bits; Mr. Taylor kept up at the top of his voice a stream of directions; and every mother's son of the attendant

A BUSINESS DEAL

heathen sprang on his pony with a yell and rode up alongside to lash at the team with his quirt and so kept them moving. For a few yards away we'd go, Charlie stoically holding the wheel and everything making a noise but the engine.

During one of the moments of comparative quiet, while the Navajos were dismounting for another push, the old gentleman explained that he was telling them to urge the ponies to their utmost until we came to a long down slope. After giving the car a start down the hill, they would hear the engine speak, "put, put", many times. They were then to jerk out the knot that held the rope around the axle and get out of the road so the car could go on. However, they were to keep up as best they could until we reached the Covered Water trading post, lest the car should stop again.

It all seemed a great lark to the Indians, who pushed and yelled and rode around us in circles, as the poor little team stood stock-still or struggled along, pulling that unnatural wagon.

The unhitching was repeated half a dozen times when there was no occasion for it, but when the engine did start, the Indians were so excited and Mr. Taylor yelled so many orders at them that the ponies were almost exhausted keeping ahead of the car before some one had presence of mind enough to untie the rope that held the doubletrees and let them drop on the horses' heels. Charlie jerked the car clear of the road and its tangle of Indians; around the bewildered ponies we bounced and down the hill we went like a torpedo, a stream of blue smoke in our rear.

Behind the smoke, with shrieks and yells, quirts lashing, came the riders. One fellow on a beautiful pinto kept his pony's nose almost against the back of the car until we reached the trading post. It was a long run for any horse and the pinto was in a lather while all the others were miles behind when we stopped.

Teddy-Witte, when I went down to their corral, were overjoyed to see me, and their enthusiasm made up for the lack of demonstration on Ken's part.

Mr. Wolfer, standing behind my chair, with a cockney accent and his thumb in the gravy, gave us a lunch of canned tomatoes, canned peaches, some sort of stewed meat and baking-powder biscuits.

I knew that situation could not last, for Ken did not care for biscuits; and I noticed that he ate soda crackers from the store stock. Once he gave me a glance that made me feel to blame because there was no bread on the table.

After the lunch the men talked business, Mrs. Gray slept, and I wandered about outside, thinking about those biscuits, the busy comings and goings at Lugontale and the stillness here. When Mr. Taylor called me to start back, I said I was not going. That started the old gentleman on another stream of Indian, Spanish and English; Ken said nothing, but his one glance meant more to me than all of Mr. Taylor's protests and explanations.

I did not go.

V · HOME

Navajo Pawn

THAT night when Mr. Wolfer had gone down to the corral to sleep, Ken explained that he was no help at all. He could not do things on time, could not remember directions and was entirely unreliable. Now that I had come, Wolfer should leave on a load of freight the next day.

The following morning as he blacked the stove and scrubbed the living-room floor for the last time — and the first — Mr. Wolfer told me the story of his life. He was a small, wiry, rat-faced, unhealthy-looking person with no "aitches" and a way of ending every speech with "Sir, to you, sir", or "Ma'am, to you, ma'am." If Ken spoke to him, he touched his forehead quickly with a "Sir, to you, sir." I found him humble and lowly to exasperation.

He told me his father was English and his mother Hindu. He had been educated in a Masonic school in India, had been cabin boy and galley cook in freighters in the South China Sea, and finally was the only survivor of a crew of a boat that went down somewhere off Southern California. He vowed then he'd get as far as possible from salt water; and I immediately admitted to myself that he had succeeded.

A missionary to the Navajos had encouraged him to marry a Navajo schoolgirl, but after some six years the missionary left and the girl's people told her to drive him out. Now he lamented because she kept the sewing machine and the cookstove; the sewing machine didn't matter so much, but he could have used the cookstove. Their little girl was in the Indian school at Fort Defiance, where he was permitted to visit the child only two or three times a year.

I was feeling sorry for the poor little rat when I was attracted by angry-sounding words in the store. I looked in. An Indian was standing one side of the counter and Ken the other. I could not understand the Indian and Ken spoke so low I couldn't hear what he said; but it was clear something was wrong, very wrong.

Spread out on the counter on Ken's right were dozens of pawned necklaces; on the Indian's right was a pile of silver dollars. The Navajo was waving his arm over the beads and shaking his head. A little group of Indians in the middle of the floor was not missing a thing, and others of their ilk were arriving. It was evident the chief actor had brought money to redeem his pawned necklace and Ken could not find the necklace.

Ken told me later that the Indian was calling him a liar and a thief and several other things much more uncomplimentary, to the Navajo's way of thinking.

There was a tautness visible, even under their blankets, in the bodies of those who were audience, and the tension in the air shut up even Wolfer's volubility. I felt a cramp in the pit of my stomach. Ken's face was expressionless. I wondered if he had a gun under the counter. If he had, and worse came to worst, there would be as many dead Indians as bullets in the gun; but, even so, would we ever leave the reservation alive? Was this the way the long journey and our new business were to end? Looking at the tense bodies, illogically I recalled the yelling, laughing crowd that had pushed the car.

"Hi-yi!" The Navajo teamster with whom Wolfer was to go yelled from outside. Ken said to the Indian, "I will finish the freighter's load. When he has gone, you and I will go through all the beads again."

The Indian joined the group in the center of the room and they bent their heads together. A minute and then all went out. Ken picked up Mr. Wolfer's overcoat and suit case, which were ready to go on the load. He scarcely had them in his hands when he gave one quick look toward the living room. Mr. Wolfer had begun anew telling me his life story as he washed the breakfast dishes. I was between him and Ken, so that neither of them could see the other without moving.

Setting the suit case down, Ken reached into a pocket

of the overcoat and drew out a handful of beads and bracelets. So quickly I was hardly sure what he did, he dropped them on some sacks of flour and pulled an empty sack over them.

Behind me Wolfer was talking about his little girl and beginning to move around, as he set the dishes on the shelf. Any step might bring him where he would see Ken. Ken dropped the coat across the suit case, gave me a glance and went outside. In another minute he came quietly into the living room from the tent and began to talk naturally to Wolfer about something in the tent. They stepped out there and I jumped toward the coat and suit case.

I felt suffocated and wondered if my hands were trembling so much I couldn't work fast. Ken would keep Wolfer out of sight, but if an Indian should come in and see me taking silver jewelry out of Wolfer's suit case, he would think we were stealing and Wolfer was getting things out of the country for us.

I pulled things from the coat pockets and thrust them under piles of calico. Then I put the suit case behind a pile of hundred-pound sacks of sugar and opened it. It was packed full of new goods from the shelves, silk scarfs, stick candy, chewing gum and dollars worth of jewelry. I dragged everything out on the floor, seized three or four cans of tomatoes to make weight, rolled them in an empty flour sack, put them in the suit case and put some shirts and socks on top. I was breathing fast and trembling, but to my surprise, when I called to Ken that the teamster was waiting for Mr. Wolfer, my voice was natural.

HOME

Ken and Mr. Wolfer came in, Wolfer telling how sorry he was to leave us. He climbed up on the load and Ken handed him his suit case and overcoat.

The load moved away from the door and Ken began to talk to the Indians outside. I gathered the jewelry we had collected into a box and placed it under the counter. On top of it, to create the appearance that the jewelry had been hidden under them, I placed some bundles of pawn tied in squares of calico.

Ken and the Indians came in and Ken pretended to look again through the necklaces that hung in the cabinet back of the counter.

The Navajo sulked and muttered things.

"But you say none of these are yours," Ken remarked, as if nothing mattered much. "Here is a box of stuff the man who kept the store before me left under the counter. See if your beads are here."

He pulled out the box and set it on the counter. The Indian found his lost beads, paid the money to redeem them and went away happy.

"The Little Crank," Ken described the Indian's disposition and stature. "I am more relieved than he is that he found his beads; traders have left the reservation, suddenly, for less — "

Ken went on to explain that under ordinary conditions, an Indian did not hesitate to kill a trader and rob and burn down the store, if the trader could not produce on demand articles the Navajo had pawned. Our situation had an added element of risk because the man who had had the store before us, a Mexican, was not popular with the Indians. The bad name of the place went back even farther than the Mexican. With their threats and thieving and petty quarreling that always killed trade and left no profit for the storekeeper, the Indians had driven out several traders.

Our speculation as to what Mr. Wolfer thought when he opened the suit case and found the tomatoes lightened the situation somewhat. Later we found out that he was an opium addict.

Our Home

With Wolfer off and yeast set for bread, I could inventory the place that was to be home.

The store was a two-room shack made of one layer of rough boards set on end and held together by a horizontal strip of box boards at top and bottom. Battens covered the cracks. The main room was the store, and before this was a platform where the freight wagons could load and unload. A partition with a doorway but no door separated our place of business from the one living room. In this I found some dirty furniture and a pile of dry-goods boxes.

The back door of the living room opened into a tent, where I found pelts of dried goat, horse and cow hides, a barrel of kerosene, and two frames to hold wool sacks upright while they were being filled.

I walked through the living room and the store, empty now except for Ken, who was arranging twenty-five-pound sacks of flour, to the freight platform. Black Mountain on the horizon seemed threatening. I tried to trace the road, forty miles of it to Lugontale and another sixty-five to Gallup and the railroad, but I could see only a yard or two of it on the tops of the humpy little hills or in the breaks in the scrubby piñons. It was a big country — and getting bigger every minute. There was not a moving thing in sight. And here Ken and I would try to earn again that feeling that something belonged to us. How we would have to stand by each other!

Ken came out and stopped behind me. I knew he would not be lonely but somehow I turned and held out my hand to him. His eyes looked puzzled and he did not take my hand; I turned back to the desert. It was bigger than ever and lonesomer; but suddenly Ken's arms were about me and he said in my ear, "There are two of us, my girl." Then he was gone into the store.

I stood still, but the desert was not lonely. And how interesting! I wanted to walk or ride in every direction.

That evening Ken and I sat either side of our table and pretended to read. The uncurtained windows looked black in the dimly lit room; and there were no sounds, either strange or familiar.

I was feeling sure there was not another human being in the world when shoes scuffed loudly on the platform outside.

With a quick gesture, Ken picked up the lamp and went into the store. I was alone in the dark and that could not last. I followed Ken.

He put the lamp on the counter and unlocked the door. An Indian in white man's clothes, but wearing a heavy turquoise-set bracelet and rings, came straight to the stove.

"Hello," he said in English.

Ken leaned on the counter; I leaned on the shelves behind it; we all stared at each other in the dim lamplight.

"I'll work for you at the store," our visitor smiled. "And I can interpret for you when you trade with Navajos. I work for traders — lots." He looked from Ken to me and I looked from him to Ken.

"Your name?" Ken asked in English, when I was thinking he would speak in Navajo to show our caller his services as interpreter would not be needed.

"John Mitchell. My father's house is down the wash from here. He is Hosteen Japon." He reached across the counter to the hollowed stone bowl that held smoking tobacco. "Give me some cigarette papers," he ordered. I did not move; but Ken quietly handed him the papers, and he rolled a cigarette and lit it with a match Ken tossed to him. My dislike for John Mitchell was increasing. I liked better those who had helped push the car; and the Little Crank who had been so angry and threatening over the loss of his beads commanded more respect than this hulk in white man's clothes.

"I'll take two of those cans of tomatoes and a sack of flour down to my mother's hogan," he informed us. "I'll be working here soon and will pay for them when you pay me." With a grand air, he lighted a second cigarette from the first.

I wanted to throw the tobacco bowl at him. Ken did not move as he answered, "You can leave your bracelet for the tomatoes and flour. Don't spend your wages until you are hired."

"Then I can't go to work to-morrow morning?"

80

"No, nor the next morning. But if you will bring a load of wood, I'll pay you."

"Hunh," our visitor snarled. "I don't cut wood. I do store work," and out he stalked.

"School man," Ken sneered, as he locked the door and I picked up the lamp.

The next morning before the room was really light, a tapping on the window on the outside of the house brought me straight up in bed, one hand reaching for Ken's shoulder. Peering in the window was a Navajo.

Ken did not open his eyes but said in Navajo, "*At-tah* (Wait). He's in a hurry to get in," Ken yawned, "but he'll be an hour buying a can of tomatoes after he gets in."

Sure enough, that Navajo stood around half the morning. So did a dozen or fifteen more, but they made it clear they did not like us. Even I could see that we were held to blame for everything that had ever gone wrong at that store.

One old sister, she must have been in her sixties, sat down on the floor against the counter, wrapped her robe tightly about her and glowered for hours. Compared to her, the others seemed actually friendly.

I found a roll of common building paper in the tent and decided I could paper our walls with it by fastening it in place with battens split from box boards. Naturally such battens were crooked; but I put a few extra waves in them, splitting them with a butcher knife, while that she-devil watched me.

I couldn't let her think the waves were due to anything but the grain of the wood, so I whistled as I worked and earned a glance of approval from Ken, as he talked with the Indians or sold an occasional nickel's worth.

By noon I was worn out, more with the strain of appearing unnoticing than with work; and Ken sent Robert, another school man, to help me. I was glad that John Mitchell did not appear but was not surprised when Robert told me the old woman on the floor was Mitchell's mother, Mrs. Japon.

Robert would not have been an addition to a paper-hanger's or carpenter's union, but we did finish the papering. The effect was rather pleasing if I shut my eyes so I could not see the general roughness. The room was warmer too, and with an Arizona blizzard outside that was a consideration.

That evening, with our unfriendly visitors shut out, Ken helped arrange the furniture. The table we placed flush with the door into the store, next to that the sewing machine, then the dressing table, made of dry-goods boxes nailed to the wall, and next a window seat which was another goods box. We fitted the bed into a corner and put the trunk at its foot. This brought us to the tent door. On the other side of that was the stove, the wood box and another window. My work shelf was under the window. Every article touched every other one.

At last, everything placed, we stood admiring our four dining chairs of hand-turned maple with rawhide seats. They had the look of Old Spain about them.

"There's space in the middle of the room for a rocking chair if I put the rockers under the bed," I planned.

HOME

"I'll put up packing boxes for dishes, get white oilcloth for the work shelf and hemstitch some of the inside sugar sacks to curtain the dish boxes. That old beggar that watched me all day —— "

"She's no beggar," Ken said quickly. "The social rank of an Indian woman is indicated by the number of skirts she wears, the number of necklaces, bracelets and rings, and the buttons on her moccasins."

"She's not much then," I answered, "four strings of shell beads, two skirts, one bracelet —— "

"And you haven't even these," Ken pointed out.

"Except the skirt," I defended myself.

"In her eyes, you don't rate," he grinned and added soberly, "But even if she has little jewelry, the others listen to her."

"Do you suppose," I began — but there was no use supposing. We would just have to wait, so we started that by going to bed.

My lack of Navajo words kept me from being of use in the store and I could hemstitch curtains and count the Indians who traded with Ken. They were painfully easy to count.

One day, when I was down on my knees scrubbing the living-room floor, I noticed the room seemed dark and I looked up to see a row of eyes above the window sill. By standing on the earth embankment outside and holding on to the window ledge, the Navajos could just see in. I had thought of asking Ken to heap the embankment higher for warmth, but then I decided to let it settle another three or four inches.

I called Ken to come look, but he was not in the least

indignant or even surprised. At first I was always forgetting that he had known people like these before I met him.

Every day, regardless of storm, Mrs. Japon arrived at the store to watch me with eyes that were snappy and keen in that face of severe unsmiling lines.

Another woman about Mrs. Japon's age I liked at once. Her voice was gentle and her smile sweet. She and her husband, with a flock of well-mannered, well-dressed children and grandchildren, lived on the piñon hill north of the store. We called them simply the Old Lady and the Old Man.

At once it was evident that she and Mrs. Japon were enemies. They did not speak, but each very apparently talked about the other. When the Old Lady patted my arm, because I guessed rightly that *chillichee* was tomatoes, Mrs. Japon left the store with ugly words snapping from the corners of thin, straight lips.

For a week after our arrival the Navajos came in increasing numbers to loaf around our big stove. When the Old Lady and her family bought from us, some others did likewise; but most rode through real winter weather to a store fifteen miles away to trade.

Ken was silent as always and I could not tell if he worried, but often there was a cramp in the pit of my stomach. If we failed here, what would we do?

Then one morning not a Navajo appeared. Was this simply scorn, I wondered, or was there really to be a move against us?

Ken and I washed the show case and put out the brightest silk scarfs for head bandeaus.

HOME

Ken said the storm was over and I said the air was so clear that Black Mountain seemed to be in our dooryard, and how far was it really?

I scrubbed the living-room floor and started to wash some blankets. Ken came to help, and that scared me still more, because he never hunted jobs just to keep busy so he couldn't think. If he had not always kept his guns loaded, I really don't know whether he would have loaded them that day.

We locked up that night as usual, though there was nothing to lock out but the wind — and the next morning the heathen were back. No one seemed concerned about anything, Ken fitted into the picture perfectly, and I tried to.

Water Rights

We were locking up one night when John Mitchell and his mother insisted on coming in. At least, she insisted and he came.

The four of us leaned across the rude counter, Ken and I on our side and Mrs. Japon and her big son opposite. Ken pushed the store tobacco bowl forward with interested hospitality.

Mrs. Japon let a long blue whiff of smoke out between tight lips and squinted at me. I felt the need of silver beads or buttons, a string of coral, anything that would make my living of importance. I turned up the coal-oil lamp. She finished her cigarette and grunted as much as to say, "Well, they'll know what I think when I'm through, anyway."

Then she began to talk, in Navajo, of course. Her glance traveled from Ken to her son and back, with only an occasional superior flash at me. Had I a single silver button in sight? And besides, I couldn't understand, anyway, and she knew it.

Ken and John Mitchell looked wise and attentive, grunted politely every few minutes and listened without moving.

Mostly I watched the face of John Mitchell. It was plain he had heard it all before and had come along only in case Ken did not understand.

The talk came very fast and straight. Ken's face did not reveal whether he understood, but I was sure he knew enough Navajo to get most of it. When at last the old woman stopped, she gave Ken and me a final glower and looked at her son. John squirmed a little and began to talk. It occurred to me that if he had stayed at home with his mother, instead of going to school, she would have made more of a man of him.

What he said was in fairly good accent. "My mother she say the water will cost you one hundred dollars. It is the price of the water from the spring at the bottom of the dry wash. You have seen. You get water there, you and your horses. She say that the traders that come to this place always owe her for the water. She say pay now."

It had taken his mother at least ten minutes to say as much. I feared John had omitted something, the best part perhaps.

A hundred dollars! It was more than Ken and I had seen in many a day. What would Ken do?

He turned to John and spoke slowly in English, as if he had not understood much of the lady's tirade.

"A hundred dollars for the water?"

John nodded.

"How long since you received this hundred dollars?"

"A year ago. It is a year since that other trader came here. He pay in food and cloth. She say you pay that way too."

To give Ken more time, I moved the lamp and put more matches where our guests could reach them.

He did not hesitate. "I paid that other trader for everything he had here, and he had paid for the water, so I expected to use it as he had."

Taking much too long for such a short speech, it seemed to me, John repeated this to his mother.

She did not let him finish but let out a squeal of rage and leaned across the counter, her arms outstretched and her bony fingers clutching fiercely. And how she talked! Her face was dark, veins stood out on her forehead and sweat streaked down her face from the edge of her hair.

We listened quietly until she stopped for breath, when John said calmly, "She say all that same things over again. She say it very hard. She say too the *deneh* on the piñon hill are not to use this water."

We knew the people on the piñon hill were the Old Lady's family.

"My mother is angry," Ken spoke gently, but I knew from his tone that we would discuss no more business that night. "We will talk about water another time. Now you may trade on a blanket you will make for me, a blanket worth five dollars." He turned to the shelves. "What will it be, my mother? You like peaches, I know, and coffee."

Ken began to put cans and packages down on the counter before Mrs. Japon. At first she sulked, but as he filled a bag with peanuts and stick candy and said, "This for the children at your home," she unbent and, taking the shawl from her shoulders, spread it on the counter and piled the packages on it, ordered an additional sack of flour, tied the corners of her shawl and slung the load to her back and turned to the door. As her educated son followed her, with one sweep of his arm he gathered up all the matches from the stone bowl.

Ken locked the door. "You'd better go and see the Old Lady in the morning. A schoolgirl niece who is visiting her will interpret for you."

I was glad enough for an excuse to go into a hogan and especially the Old Lady's. I started right after breakfast. Ken said any hour at all was visiting hour for Indians, so it could be for me too. I had studied the outside of the Navajo homes from a distance; but since they rarely built within easy sight of a road, my interest had never been satisfied.

Now, as I tramped over the piñon ridge and across a rough little mesa toward the Old Lady's hogan, I followed a narrow trail worn by human feet, not horses'. It swung in easy zigzags up the steep places, where a woman could carry a keg of water slung in a blanket on her back. Across the angles of this trail was a straight one to be used when coming downhill only, or for a stiff climb up without a load.

HOME

I expected to come upon the hogan among the trees, but it was several yards beyond the stand of scrubby cedars and piñons and near the edge of a bare slope of sandstone that dropped forty feet into a little valley below.

Because from without it was a dome of dirt the exact match of its surroundings, at a little distance it was invisible but for the curl of blue smoke coming from the top. Several yards away two other curls of smoke crept out over the low tree tops from the hogans of the married daughters, Slender Girl and Robert's wife; White Hat, the Old Lady's married son, lived not far away to the left, on the dry sand wash that led to the post; his wife also carried water from our well.

Wondering which of the three hogans I should choose, I took the nearest. The ground about it was bare; there was no wood pile, no trash or rubbish accumulation. The wagon standing near by was the only object that seemed to make a companion for the smoke.

I walked around the hogan and found the door on the east side. The house was perfectly round, the dirt surface showed impressions of a shovel blade, where the dirt had been pounded down, but there had not been the least attempt to plaster.

The doorway was a bit narrow and low; I had to stoop slightly; there was no place to knock and no door, only an old piece of canvas, a fragment of an old tent, I guessed, which hung straight down from the top beam of the door. When I drew this aside, I expected to look directly into the hogan, but two feet ahead was another curtain.

I spoke and was relieved when the Old Lady's voice said *"Haco"* (Come in), and she drew aside the curtain.

She sat next the door, before her loom. The morning sun poured through a three foot hole in the roof over the vivid pattern of the blanket. A tiny cooking fire sent out a thin gray spiral of smoke, which, as long as I stood, swirled about the hogan and made my eyes smart until I thought blindness was upon me.

The Old Lady motioned me to sit quickly on a thick sheepskin. The instant I was seated, the smoke ascended straight to the smoke hole and the air was clear; the ventilation was perfect and there was no odor of cooking or closeness.

Near the Old Lady sat her unmarried daughter, spinning. We smiled at each other, and the Old Lady spoke to three children playing with a prairie dog in the back of the room. They all looked quite at home and friendly and unembarrassed. One of the children went out quietly and I motioned to the Old Lady to go on with her work, so I could watch. It was a beautiful piece of weaving, closely done and accurate. The pattern was one of diminishing diamonds, outlined in white.

The daughter sitting on the floor, with her slender spindle whirling rapidly between her fingers, had not stopped work at all. The flat wooden disk near the lower end of the spindle had been shaped without the aid of a saw, I thought, but it was both smooth and round.

The inside of the hogan looked like an inverted basket. For three feet up from the ground the walls were of cedar posts set upright, very close together. Beginning at the top of these was a perfect dome of curved, interlapping cedar branches as large as my arm. All the cedar was peeled and beautifully smoke-stained. The edge of the smoke hole was perfectly finished.

The few household utensils — cooking pots and tin or granite-ware cups, were in a box which had once contained canned goods. Beds were apparently the sheep skins and the compact bundles of robes and cotton-filled comforts of white man's manufacture.

Unevenness in the walls provided small spaces to tuck things away; the rough knots served to hang things on; the loom was tied to overhead poles. The room had an air of spacious cleanness.

I had not nearly looked my fill when the door curtains parted and the child who had gone out entered, followed by the two married daughters, who carried spinning with them, and by the schoolgirl niece. She was dressed entirely "white": a blue wash dress, somewhat rumpled from hogan inconveniences, shoes and stockings and hair ribbons.

I held out my hand and said, "I'm happy to see you; you can help me get acquainted with your aunt here, whom I want to know better because we are to be neighbors." The girl shook hands and smiled. She spoke better English than either John Mitchell or Robert.

"We have been talking about you ever since you came to the trading post; we wondered if you would ever call at the hogans. Not many of the traders' wives do."

"I am glad to come here," I said quickly. "I will be very happy if your aunt will let me come often and watch her work."

Marie, the schoolgirl, spoke in Navajo to the Old

Lady and her daughters smiled and spoke softly and went on with their work. It was a friendly place.

The schoolgirl sat on the box that held the cooking things and said, laughing a little, "I may be Navajo, but I can't sit on the ground any more without my feet going to sleep. I work in a missionary's family near the Indian School at Ship Rock and I am to be here only a few days more. I'm glad; it's too hard to keep my clothes clean and I don't get along very well with 'blanket Indians'; I have been away too long."

There was so very much I wanted to hear that talking to some one who understood was a treat indeed. Marie stopped often to go over in Navajo what we had been saying, and the others always listened and had some comment or question that kept the conversation going briskly.

It was getting well towards noon before I could steer the talk around to the purpose of my visit; but when I did mention Mrs. Japon and the water, Marie spoke at length to the Old Lady and turned back to me.

"It was years ago. The water then ran down the dry wash between the straight-up-and-down rocks and out into the valley, where Japon's hogan stands now; but in those days Hosteen Blue Goat, my aunt's father, and all his family lived there, and they watered a little cornfield with the water and there was plenty, even though it dried up in the summer time.

"There were not so many horses then, nor so many sheep to drink the water, so there was enough for everybody and so Japon's family moved here from away on the other side of the mountain, where the water had dried up. When spring came again, they did not move back to where they came from, as they should have done; and because there was really enough water for both families, Hosteen Blue Goat said nothing and both hogans used water out of the spring for three, maybe four years. Then the dry years came again and there was not enough water; but still Japon's people took it; and Japon's family had many strong men and their women owned many sheep, and so there was a quarrel and a fight or two, and after awhile Hosteen Blue Goat's people moved away, because the others were very quarrelsome and bad, and Hosteen Blue Goat liked peace and quiet; but before they moved, Hosteen Blue Goat killed Mrs. Japon's father and his best horse besides."

By this time I was wide-eyed and gasping and thought I was not getting the story straight.

"And how many of Hosteen Blue Goat's family did the Japons kill?" I asked.

Marie and the Old Lady talked fast for several minutes.

"None," reported Marie. "It was a poor shot, they say. Too far, perhaps. It only made him limp. It was a brother of Hosteen Blue Goat; but Hosteen Blue Goat says it is not a good thing to quarrel and shoot one another, so because he did not want to do those things any more, he took his family away."

I could not help saying, "But he had the best of the fight, as well as the first right to the water. Do you think he should have taken his family and moved away?"

Marie repeated my questions to the Old Lady, who

93

smiled and answered sweetly and Marie translated again, "Hosteen Blue Goat ruled all his family — he has always been very wise — he said that some day they should all come back and live near the spring; but there must be no fighting. They came, but Mrs. Japon and my aunt do not speak to each other and my aunt sends only the children to the spring. Even Mrs. Japon would not drive a child away from the water."

The answer was conclusive. I held their hands and tried to tell them how much I wanted to be friends and went back to report to Ken.

The next morning, before any trade arrived, Ken called to me, "Come, I want to show you something." Thinking it would be something for her to bark at, Lady Betty went tearing out; and I locked the store door and followed her. Ken had a shovel and a pick and we went down the sandy slope to the spring.

The bottom of the wash was narrow and stony, with big flat steps of sandstone where the freshets had eaten down to the hard bottom. The narrow bench of sand where the old spring was located was above the level of the stony bottom of the dry stream bed itself. Ken walked around, looking at the formation, kicking at the sand and scraping on the bottom with his boot toe. Betty rushed in and began to dig wherever he started. Finally he went back to the spring and, getting down on his hands and knees, leaned over with his head fairly in the hole. I quickly got down and put my head in too, and Betty crowded in between us and looked in herself.

All the water had been dipped out the night before and not more than five inches had risen. On one side the

sandy wall showed a damp band twelve inches or so
above the water's edge; on the opposite side it seemed
to be dry to the very water. We drew our heads out and
looked at each other from our lowly positions on hands
and knees; we grinned and got up, knowing the direction of the flow of the underground water. I took the
pick and passed it to Ken. He stepped one, two, three,
four, five yards from the spring and stopped against a
rock in the very center of the wash. We dug; the sand
was easy. Ken said, "It will be hard digging after we
get down to that red hardpan, but here goes for water
and Providence."

We had worked an hour or more when two Navajos
came riding down the trail from the mountain country.
They were astonished and interested; they had seen
shovels before but evidently not a pick, and as Ken soon
demonstrated it for them, they were both eager to try
it. We all took turns. Another Indian approached; we
called him to come and see and he did. I had to go to the
store when some women came to trade, and then the
hole was three feet deep and sinking fast.

As soon as I could get away from the store, I took
some cold biscuits and a can of peaches and hurried
down the hill again, spoons, can opener and all. It was
an exciting day; we could hardly wait to see if we were
going to strike water. More Navajos arrived; every one
who came worked and every one stayed to peer down
into the well after every shovel full, to see if there was
a bit of dampness showing.

Only when it was too dark to see did they quit, and
one brought me a handful of sand from the bottom of

the ten-foot well. It was damp enough so that he could squeeze it into a moist mold of his palm. We all laughed together; they promised they would come early to-morrow and use the peculiar tool again.

Four of the Indians slept in the camp hogan near the store and before sunup were pounding on the outside of the house next our bed and shouting gleefully, *"Toh! Toh!* Come and see. Hurry! Hurry!"

Ken jumped up. "Run! They say there's water." We called to them that we were coming, that we hurried. We shouted to know how much water was in the well. "Enough for two horses, maybe three," they called back, as we pulled on our clothes as fast as we could.

At the well we all went down on our hands and knees to stare into the depths where lay, cool and clear and perfectly beautiful, that most marvelous thing on earth — water.

Willing hands brought the iron wheelbarrow to use for a watering trough and I led Teddy-Witte down for the first drink; other ponies were brought down. We had to empty the well so the men could go on digging, and there was no place to put the water unless it was in a horse; not a man there would have thought for a moment that he could have poured it on the ground.

An Indian who drove in with a wagon and some hides to sell was hustled off to haul some poles to cover the well with, when it should once be deep enough. I was sent posthaste for axes, and Betty got all wrought up because she thought I had lost my mind and was going too, and leave her and Ken by the well.

The pails full of dirt, rocks and muddy water came

up hand over hand to be dumped on a rock basin where the sand could be scraped away and the water settle, so that a horse might drink.

There was coffee and bread and meat and canned tomatoes for every one at noon. The load of poles came, crooked sticks of hard tough cedar. Here the Indians took the work away from Ken, as they were working with something they understood now. They went at it as if they were roofing a hogan. Of course they left a hole in the center and here Ken set a curb made of an Arbuckle's coffee case with leather hinges on a lid and a hasp and padlock. I brought a brand-new galvanized iron well bucket and a length of new rope.

Ken explained that any one who came would be welcome to fill a keg or a canteen or to water a thirsty horse, for this water was the old, old spring that belonged to Hosteen Blue Goat and that we should all know this and call it his Covered Water.

The Old Lady and her father, Hosteen Blue Goat, came, and Ken unlocked the well so they could look in.

Blue Goat drank deeply from a tin can and declared, "It is beautiful; it is my old spring that you have brought back again; this is as it was when I was young. That other hole there — it is not."

All those who had helped with the digging felt friendly and acquainted and ceased to ride fifteen miles to the Saluni post to trade.

VI · INDIAN WAYS AND WILES

THOUGH Mrs. Japon scolded because she did not receive the hundred dollars for water used at the store, she could not complain long in the general atmosphere of good will and soon seemed satisfied with the exclusive use of water from the spring she claimed.

I was beginning to know a little what to expect from the Indians, and, of necessity, I learned rapidly the Navajo words for articles in the store. Our customers enjoyed teaching me and would point to sugar, coffee, tobacco, pants and repeat endlessly, *eshinlcaon, co-weh, natoh, clagi-e,* until I could say them with some shadow of the correct accent.

The terms for money were the hardest for me; but the Indians were one hundred per cent. good as beggars, and it was the lingo with which they tried to wheedle us out of everything movable on the place that I first learned.

"My dear grandmother," one would begin. "Come into this corner with me. We will speak slowly and not get mad. The children at my house who call you mother are hungry. They cry and call for candy and bread. One has a stomach. He said his mother would send medicine and apples and candy to him by me. Your children need shoes. In six months I will cut my wool. Allow me, my mother, my sister, my pretty younger sister, to owe you twenty dollars until I shear my sheep. This will make all your children who live at my house warm.

"Other Navajos may lie to you and never pay their bills, but I am not like those crows and coyotes and gamblers. I never lie; I do not know anything about cards; I never go where cards are. I work at home — haul wood, shear sheep, and look after my cattle that these thieves of gamblers do not steal them or eat them.

"See. My coat is worn out and no good. Let me have a new coat. Let me owe you four dollars for a new coat. Is this one four dollars? It is very thin and ugly for four dollars. But I am poor, so I will take it. And some shoes? My feet are wet and cold. How much for these shoes? Three-fifty? Oh, my mother, let me have them for three dollars. See, they are poor ugly things. Three dollars is lots for them. And you must give me a pair of socks for friendship, because I am your very good friend. I tell all Navajos how nice you are, how you feed any one who asks it and give apples and candy to all the

children who come to your store. All trails, everywhere,
lead to your store. The Indians all say you are good. Put
some sweets in a bag, and I will take it to your children
and tell them their mother sent it.

"Is this good flour? It looks black; it may be wormy.
Give me a knife and I will cut open the sack and look at
it. My wife will be mad if I bring poor flour. You use
it? Is this what you make bread of? Bring me a piece of
the bread. Maybe you lie. The bread is good. May I see
the sack you used? I can tell by the picture on the flour
sack if you are lying about the bread.

"How much do I owe you now? Twenty dollars, plus
four, plus three-fifty? Twenty-seven fifty? I will trade
two-fifty more and then I will remember, thirty dollars.
I never could remember twenty-seven fifty.

"In fifteen days my wife will bring you a blanket.
The blanket is big and will be worth ten dollars, maybe
twelve. It would bring fifteen dollars at Chin Lee, but
my wife will bring it here and take twelve dollars because you are her sister. And my wife wants any empty
lard pails you have. Bring me the one I see on your shelf
now.

"Have you a sack? What shall I carry all this stuff
home in? Give me a sack, mother, a poor ugly gunny
sack will do. None? Then I must use my robe and I will
be cold riding.

"Give me some strong twine to tie this robe so I won't
lose my sack of flour. More than that, make it strong
enough for a hair string. See, my hair string is dirty. I
need a new one.

"It's a long way to my house and my horse is tired.

While he rests I have time to eat. Give me a can of pears
and a box of crackers, because I live a long way off and
come all this distance in the cold to trade with you because I know you are good and we are friends. That's
right, that's good. This is for friendship. My mother
doesn't want money for this, because she feeds her
friends. Have you any coffee made? No? Then bring me
a cup of water and pass me a spoon and a can opener.
May I have the spoon? Your little boy that lives at our
house lost the best spoon we had. I'll take this one.
Thanks, my mother, good, good. Now I go."

We Make a Friend

The snow fell and melted. It rained and a freezing
wind made the trails glassy. The post was on sandy soil,
but our freight teams dragged through clay between
our hills and Lugontale.

One morning when the wind and snow made trails
slippery and riding cold, an Indian we had never seen
before came in with a boy about nine years old. They
said nothing but stood by the stove, warming themselves. The icy wind that blew through the house when
they entered sent me to fill the stove again. We looked
one another over in a friendly way, and I put my hand
on the child's ruddy cheek.

He was cold as stone and dressed in blue denim overalls and a worn velvet shirt. His hair was matted and
wind-blown, and clay was caked on his overalls.

"Hosteen Untiligi", the other Indians in the store
called the stranger. When Ken asked where his hogan

was, he replied that it was near Saluni. This was another trading post fifteen miles away.

"It is a cold day for the child to ride," Ken said.

"Yes, cold. That is why we came. We are looking for a coat for him. I have promised him a coat to wear. Let us see a small coat. The store at Saluni has no small coats, so we came here."

Ken translated and I went to the shelves, praying there would be a very small coat. Men's sizes only. I was as disappointed as the child. He stared across the picket gate that barred customers from the shelves and pointed bashfully.

"The gray one — I like the gray one. Let me have it in my hand."

Again Ken translated what I did not understand, and I took the coat from the pile and held it up for him to see that it was big enough for his father.

"Too bad," I said. "See, it is for a man, not a little boy."

The child turned to his father, "I want the gray coat," he said.

Every one in the store became concerned. "But it is so big," they told him.

He looked straight at his father and repeated, "I want the gray coat. I want it on now."

Thinking to prove to him once and for all that he did not want the big coat, I took it through the gate into the "bull-pen", as Ken inelegantly called the customer's area, and held it for the boy to put his thin little arms into the sleeves. The bottom of the coat came down to his ankles. His little tousled black head and earnest brown face looked too comical, and we all burst out laughing; but he only turned round and round, trying to see himself. Then he stood before his father and drew his arms tight across in front, the ends of the long sleeves dangling a foot beyond his little hands.

"It is warm," he said. "I want the gray coat."

The man looked helpless. It was plain to see it would be hard to get the coat away from the boy now.

Some one suggested that the sleeves be cut off so that he could use his hands, at least. It was an idea and a knife was produced.

The father turned to me, asked, "How much is the coat?" and took a handful of silver dollars from his pocket.

The boy gave his father a joyful glance and held out his arms to the man who had the knife ready. I stopped them.

"Let me," I said. "If you really want the coat, let me cut off the sleeves and sew them up right."

That pleased everybody. "The white woman will fix it; she has a needle," they told each other. Because Navajo men often made their own shirts, they understood what I would do to fix the sleeves. I went for the scissors, some pins, and with everybody's help I measured and marked the coat for alterations on sleeves and shoulders. We lapped it over and made a double-breasted coat of it; we took up the fullness in the back seam. Then, with the garment over my arm, I went into my own room and with some misgivings I ripped and basted.

Every one waited, and between stretches on the sew-

ing machine, I heard some scraps of talk I understood.
"She is a friend to *deneh* [Navajos]." "She likes small
boys." "She is a grandmother to your small son, my
friend."

I never was much of a seamstress and certainly not
a tailoress, but I worked and prayed the coat would
please them. If it did, we had made not one friend, but
many; if it did not, I had perhaps destroyed their slight
confidence in us and ruined a five-dollar coat.

Finally I sewed on the last button and took the coat
out. Beaming, the boy slipped his arms into the sleeves.

There were loud cries of admiration. "It is beautiful;
it is just right!" "Now the little man will be warm."

"*A-la-honi*, our grandmother has made good work on
the big coat."

The boy's father paid the five dollars most willingly.
We were all happy.

I was glad no one but the blessed and appreciative
heathen had seen the garment. It was terrible; but they
liked it and they loved me for doing it. I wanted nothing else.

Death — and More Business

Everything in sight from my window was up or down
a steep, short hill; this made the view so confusing that
I had a sort of fascinated dread of missing something that
might come up out of a hollow, if I'd only look an instant longer. I washed dishes at the work shelf and
gazed out the window until the Indian women in the
store went outside and around the house, to see what
I was watching.

INDIAN WAYS AND WILES

From the first I could not make out where the wagon road went over its hill, so I made occasion to walk that way; but when I looked out of the window again, it was gone and I could see nothing but the humping little hills tiered up to make a big one and all covered with scraggy cedar, piñon and yucca.

The whole country was bare rocks, sand and scrub pine; the smell of the sage was in our nostrils; we saw the sunsets of the mesa country and bluffs purple in the twilight.

On the Oregon Coast, one of the places where chance and Ken had landed us, the sea breezes lifted whitecaps on the water, rustled the fern and roared in the big trees. In Eastern Oregon the wind was chiefly indicated by the haystacks sailing away in fragments and the tall poplars leaning toward Perkinses. In Imperial Valley the pepper trees flounced their skirts up and down; the date palms swayed stiffly and the chickens that took the wrong tack got the gale under their wings and were carried half across the yard. I could see the wind blow in those places.

It blew at Black Mountain, but without any evident results. The stubby little trees were too stiff to move much and the ground was too wet for dust. The Indians wrapped their blankets so tightly they couldn't flap. There was nothing else but rocks.

But the very unfamiliarity of everything aroused my curiosity and held my interest.

We had been at the store two months. The Indians seemed more friendly and our trade and my vocabulary had increased to where I was useful in the store, when late one afternoon Mr. Taylor and a government man named Dean drove up in a noisy Ford.

After supper I took care of the trade while the men talked in the living room. I supposed that the visit had to do with our license to trade with the Indians.

The wind was wailing around the building and fine snow began to sift in through the spaces where the roof and wall did not meet. I spread empty sacks over the piled bags of sugar to catch the drifted snow, and asked some of the Indians standing about to bring in more wood to keep the stove hot. We all listened to the murmur of the men's voices in the other room. A government official did not visit outlying trading posts every day or for nothing; but the storm was so noisy that I could not catch the words in the next room, hard as I strained my ears.

Suddenly the door flew open and a swirl of snow and fresh air puffed in. Slender Girl slipped inside and leaned against the door, her hair blown wildly above her shawl; she looked ghastly. I could hardly believe my eyes, for I had seen her laughing only that morning.

Every man in the store turned and looked at her. She was breathing deeply and fast. "I want a robe," she said. Hosteen Tso drew off his own robe and held it out to her, another stepped up and handed her his. She took them both, opened the door, let in another cloud of snow and was gone.

I had a glimpse of two children on ponies outside, as Hosteen Nez Begay jumped to push the door shut against the wind.

I started hastily around the counter but before I reached the door Nez Begay held me back.

"Don't go out there," he said. "She has what she came for; she is taking the children up to Hosteen Blue Goat's hogan."

I stopped, looking from face to face. "What is it?" I asked. "She looked ill. Is there trouble? She is my friend; let me go to her."

"No," said a half dozen voices.

Nez Begay still held me and Hosteen Tso explained. "There is nothing for you to do now; wait a few days and you can help her. Did you not know? Her sister, Robert's wife, died at sundown. There is nothing you can do until things are taken care of by her father, Blue Goat. In four days they will come to you because you are their grandmother."

Stunned, I went back behind the counter. I had been laughing with the Old Lady and her daughters only that morning over a baby dress that I had made for the prospective arrival at Robert's hogan. They had cut it out for me because I did not know how to make clothes for a Navajo baby. It had a waistband and a tiny plaited skirt and a little waist with sleeves; it was like a doll's dress. I had told the Old Lady so and we had laughed happily together over it.

I turned to Nez Begay and asked, "Did the baby live?"

A half dozen answered me, "Yes — yes; it is a boy, a big fine boy, and it lives; it will be all right; its grandmother will take care of it; she will make it live and grow; she understands small babies."

Every one seemed confident of that, at least; but a damper had been put on the evening and even their curiosity about Mr. Dean could not keep them any longer. The two men who had given away their robes went out with the rest into the cold and storm.

We made beds on top of the wide counter for Mr. Taylor and Mr. Dean, and the thin walls and doorless condition of our sleeping quarters made it impossible to hold any private conference after retiring; but Ken did explain that Robert very likely would go to his mother's hogan on the other side of the mountains for a time and that he would have no claim to the baby. It belonged to the dead wife's family.

After an early breakfast we watched the Ford rattle out of sight.

Ken turned to me and spoke casually, "You won't need to worry now. Dean gave me the contract to furnish beef to the Indian Schools where they keep Indian children nine months of the year. I've been thinking we might buy that farm next to old Kit Barton's on the river."

"Ken," I gasped and grabbed him.

He held me close for a minute. "Kit will make the deal for us if we ask him."

"A farm," I gasped. "A home of our own — and you let me sleep without telling me."

"It'll mean our noses on the grindstone," Ken cautioned.

But he could not frighten me with work. "If it means our whole faces, who cares?"

Trade began then and there was little chance to talk.

"That house was adobe, wasn't it?" I asked, as I cut plug tobacco for Hosten Tso.

Ken nodded.

"Four rooms or five?" I asked an hour later.

"Five," he replied, as he explained to Hosteen Cla that he would buy the red steer with one horn and the two white spots on his back. For the rest of the day there was no more of even this scrappy talk; but that evening, when the Navajos were shut out and we sat beside the lamp on our one and only table, I brought out pencil and paper and we made plans and added figures until midnight. Dairy cattle, we decided on, and white chickens and grapes and a garden. It seemed like paradise we were planning. When we slept, I dreamed of feeding grapes to red steers in my five-room house, and the steers had eyes like Mrs. Japon.

Red Blood

We tried to do the butchering as early as possible. This meant that Ken had to be at the corral as soon as there was daylight enough to make the sights on his rifle visible. It was a sort of game to see how much we could get done before an Indian arrived; but if they had seen the steer in the corral the night before, invariably a reception committee of Navajo women would be waiting for him beside the gate.

What time they left home I could not guess.

If they had not happened to see cattle in the corral, the high thin pop of the rifle would be answered from the nearest hogans, a yodel-like call that brought the Navajos quirting furiously to the killing to throw themselves from their ponies and run to the corral, demanding sharp knives so they could help.

Giving the men several moments' head start with the work, I would lock the store door and, carrying two large pans, would join the "other squaws," to watch the men finish the skinning and hoist the carcass up on the pulleys for dressing.

Not one particle was allowed to go to waste, and we learned many things in conservation from the daily customs of those who had known and handled meat since buffalo days. One woman, generally Mrs. Japon or her daughter, had hold of a horn as soon after the shot was fired as she could scamper across the corral, and never would she let go, but followed the carcass right up to the windlass and up the hoist. This meant to every one that the head was hers, after Ken was through with it. Generally she got in his way while he was skinning it, and he, with neverending patience, pushed her and her like out of the way as gently as if they were pestering children.

Even though Mrs. Japon had made the head hers by the nine points of possession, every one knew I would come with my pan for the brains and tongue. As soon as I was satisfied, she tied what was left of the head to her saddle and hurried back to the scene for more.

When my second pan was filled with the liver and abdominal fat, I asked some one to help carry the two pans to the house. An assistant appeared willingly, because I always gave her a part of the liver; but she, knowing that it was safe with me, left it until she was ready to go home and hurried back to the pen.

One day Mrs. Little Crank reached in and put her hand almost under Ken's knife. He told her to wait, and when she did not move, he turned his knife, gave her a crack across the knuckles with the back of it and went on with his work.

Her voice and her language more than equalled Mrs. Japon's at that lady's best. Her hand was covered with beef blood which she thought was her own. She held it out from her body and waited for the blood to drip, but never stopped for breath in her swearing by all the coyote, snake and bear gods that Ken had ruined his grandmother — meaning herself. Finally she wrapped the hurt hand in a corner of her shawl and stood sulking and muttering.

"Show me," I said.

She muttered and did not stir.

I insisted. At last she held out her hands and I poured water over them.

Not a cut! No blood!

Her remarks increased in tempo, pitch and volume.

By that time Mrs. Japon and daughter, the Old Lady and Charlie's wife had all the entrails.

This was too much. The air fairly crackled with Mrs. Little Crank's words; but the others, both men and women who had been quiet and abashed when they thought Ken was really angry, now broke in with hoots and laughs. A good time was had by all.

In the midst of the uproar, the Old Lady touched

my arm and pointed to Japon's wife who was standing some fifteen feet away, intent on shaking the half-digested grass from the several stomachs.

"Look, my sister, do you see where your new cow liver hangs on the fence? That she-coyote who is the wife of Japon took it. Knowing it to be your own, I would not touch it, but your husband allowed her to take it. He said no word to her, and she is a snake and a crow, and takes the liver when she knows as well as I do that it is always yours. And the fat also. She is a thief and took what was yours. She is a coyote, a she-coyote who steals and lies. For many years have I known her and always she steals and lies."

Such bitter contempt you never heard. The Old Lady, as I knew, was speaking of a lifelong enemy.

Nothing would have pleased her more than to have me run Mrs. Japon out of the corral, as the coyote the Old Lady called her; but both women, as the heads of big families, were valuable customers, and the Old Lady was a famous weaver and an asset to any store.

I took the knife to the fence where Japon's wife had hung the tallow and liver and put all the tallow and part of the liver in my pan. The thief watched and glowered at the Old Lady. Later I divided the tallow and gave some to each of them and some to Mrs. Little Crank, who was still sulking.

While some of the women turned to cutting the entrails into short lengths, splitting them and tying them into bundles, and others slit open the paunch and threw it over the fence like a saddle blanket, Japon's wife made the lungs and esophagus hers by stuffing them out of sight into a flour sack. Later, I knew she would roast them over a bed of coals until they were about the size and color of two small roast chickens. I never did taste this delicacy, but it smelled delicious.

As I watched the flour sack being fastened securely to Mrs. Japon's saddle, I did not call the others to notice that again she was getting more than her share.

The beef blood was very precious and was saved in tin cans or the coffeepot. Later, it was stirred thick with corn meal, stuffed into short lengths of the small intestine of either beef or sheep, and boiled for a long time. It was then dried and made a condensed ration the Navajos could carry easily.

I wondered if they made calves' foot jelly from the foot and shank they seemed so eager to secure. I saw one of the Old Lady's grandsons wrap a forefoot carefully in the silk handkerchief he wore about his head and tie it to his saddle.

The Tale of a Coyote

Ken added to the money that meant we could buy the farm — some day — by trapping coyotes. There was a bounty on them, and the well-dressed woman beyond those bleak Arizona hills would pay well for a coyote fur that even the poorest Navajo would not touch.

It was nearly noon one day and there were eight or ten Navajos, men and women, in the store when Ken rode up and passed the sack he used to carry the coyote skins in to me. I carried it to the backyard tent without taking it through the store. The Indians had very definite feelings about coyote skins and we were careful not to offend them. We would not stretch the skins to dry until every one was gone that evening and then would keep them inside the tent.

Ken came back from the corral and went through an elaborate washing and changed his clothes before going into the store. The Indians understood, of course, that he was removing any bad luck that might follow the handling of coyote skins, and the last performance was to have me sprinkle talcum powder over his hands. This he rubbed in lightly and turned to the store full of Indians.

"Tell me, my brothers," Ken asked, "which one of you knows coyotes well. I have seen an odd thing to-day."

They all looked at Hosteen Untiligi; and that gentleman spoke up and admitted that he knew coyotes better than most *deneh*.

"Then tell me what it means when a coyote has white hairs on the tip of his tail."

Silence; they all stared. At last John Mitchell laughed a little and said, "Maybe you did not look good; the hairs on the tip of a coyote's tail are black — always. We all know that."

"But one had white hairs," Ken insisted. "Only a few on the very tip."

Hosteen Untiligi looked soberly at Ken. "Did you say white?" He spoke unbelievingly and Ken repeated what he had just said.

"Then," stated Hosteen Untiligi, "that coyote was

no coyote but a *chindi* (devil), and you must take steps quickly to undo any mischief. This is serious."

He reached for the medicine pouch that medicine men carry on a strap across one shoulder. Hosteen Untiligi's was studded thick with silver buttons. The pouch itself was leather and made like an envelope and inside were tiny buckskin rolls or bags of corn pollen, herbs, turquoise chips, and flint arrowpoints. These he took out and I quickly lifted a bolt of calico from the shelves and tore off a shirt length, two and one-half yards, and spread it before him.

This won me an approving glance from Ken and John Mitchell said, "That is right; he is going to make medicine to take away the bad luck. You should pay him now."

Hosteen Untiligi placed all his medicines on the calico, carefully untied the tiny buckskin bag and began to sing, low. The others, some sitting on the floor, a few standing at the counter, gave him all their attention, some humming with him.

I was fascinated; here was a remedy to suit the affliction. Ken and I leaned across the counter, watching.

With thumb and finger, Hosteen Untiligi took a pinch of pollen from the little bag and on the smooth counter in front of Ken he made a tiny picture no larger than a silver dollar. He asked for salt, and in the yellow pollen and the white salt he completed the symbol.

I could not distinguish any likeness to a coyote or anything else in it, but it was painstakingly done and evidently by a known design.

As the song stopped, Hosteen Untiligi took one of the flint arrowpoints and destroyed the little picture by scraping the pollen and salt up into a pile; John Mitchell took a bit of cracker-box pasteboard from the wood box and brushed the little pile up and carried it out of doors, where he tossed it into the wind, and then came back.

"Now," said the doctor, putting his things away again into his silver-mounted pouch, "be careful in the future and send for me if you should ever see such a coyote again."

Ken assured him soberly that he would and set out canned peaches and crackers for the crowd. I went quietly into the bedroom to smile. No one else seemed to want to.

It was not only coyote skins we collected in the late winter and spring of 1915. The winter was a hard one, and Navajo sheep and goats starved. To save what they could out of the disaster, the Indians sold us the goat hides and sheep pelts. We found a ready market for them, but before they could be sent out on the freight wagons, they had to be dried and baled. And where to dry them? They accumulated so rapidly we had no space.

One day, after Ken had ridden out to bring in a red steer he had bargained for and Hosteen Japon pretended he could not find, a peck, peck, peck, again and again, began on the outside of the house.

Woodpeckers? I listened — and stepped outside.

There on a box stood the Hobo, a Navajo as destitute as a coyote and looking it. As high as he could reach and as low as he could crawl he was nailing goat hides and sheep pelts. (Why is one hides and the other pelts?) Ken's orders, of course. The walls of that shack were but one layer of boards. When the peck, peck, peck had continued until nearly noon and I knew I should go crazy if the Hobo drove another nail, he came in to ask for more. More nails! There were none closer than Lugontale, forty miles of muddy road away — and I was glad of it.

That heathen had driven a nail every two inches around every leg and tail.

When Ken returned, I remonstrated against the appearance of the outside of the house. "What's the outside of a house for?" he asked. However, the goat tail nailed to my window sill was removed, though Ken considered me queer.

It was two days later when I took my washing out to hang on the lines, that I found the Hobo had filled every bit of line with green horse and cow hides.

Later I said to Ken some things I had not said to the Hobo, because I did not know his language well enough. I knew Ken's, so I got a new clothesline.

The amazing thing about all the hides was that in the Arizona sun and wind they dried without odor.

VII · BLANKET INDIANS — AND
A "SCHOOL MAN"

THE big spring job at a Navajo trading post is receiving, weighing and shipping wool.

Indians were thick indoors and out and there was color and movement — and smell. They were pounding on our door before daylight; and, though their wool was sold and the money spent, most of them stayed in the store until they were pushed out before midnight.

They brought the wool wrapped in their robes and sewed with Yucca spines, each stitch cut and tied in a knot it was impossible to untie after the fiber dried.

The Little Crank was the first of the heathen to put rocks and sand in the wool to make it weigh heavy. When Ken threw them out he never turned a hair. "The baby threw the rocks in and the wind blows very hard in my valley. It blows the sand into the wool as you see."

Often we found *depay-be-yaas,* sheep ticks, in the wool. I found one on Ken's neck, and to the end of wool season he thought he was covered with them.

From the first it struck me how primitive the method of handling the wool was as compared with that of handling raw cotton in the Imperial Valley. A wool sack, about seven feet long, was fastened to a hoop which kept the sack open. The hoop was suspended on a framework high enough so the bottom of the sack just touched the ground, the black and the white wool in separate sacks; and in each stood a Navajo who tramped the wool down as it was thrown in.

Though John Mitchell was the typical spoiled eldest son, with a few characteristics peculiar to himself and some even less desirable added by white man's training, we needed help with the wool and Ken employed him. John knew enough English so that we counted on him to understand what we said, only to find later he hadn't understood, — or pretended he hadn't.

One rushing day, when two or three ponies were tied to every piñon tree near the store and Ken was making friends with a man who had many sheep and would therefore be a valuable customer, I was trying to handle the brisk wool trade alone without disturbing Ken.

John was in the tent weighing wool as the Navajos brought it to him. He scratched the amount each Indian had on a scrap of paper, and when this was given to me, I paid for the amount indicated.

The figures grew larger, — ten pounds, twenty-five, fifty, sixty. When wool is as hard to compress and wrap in a compact package as feathers, I couldn't see how sixty pounds could be rolled into a bundle and tied behind a saddle.

I looked for Ken. He and the stranger were entering the store. I edged nearer. "You have a beautiful horse," Ken was saying. "He is a strong horse. Some day — ," I stepped back to the trading. This was no time to interrupt.

But the next paper was marked one hundred pounds.

Ken and his friend were leaning against the counter by the stone tobacco bowl. I touched Ken on the shoulder and showed him the slip of paper. "Can a hundred pounds of wool be rolled in a blanket and tied at each end like a tamale?" Ken looked at me a second and went himself to weigh the wool. It checked just forty pounds and was a big, awkward bundle at that.

"We won't need you any more to-day," he told John Mitchell; and John showed his nice white teeth in a pleasant grin and sauntered out of the wool tent and into the store.

The store was full of Indians and I was struggling to concentrate on the job of remembering what every person's every nickle and dime had gone for, and just how much each had spent and what was left.

"Maybe you want me to help you trade," John offered generously. "I know all about cash registers and measuring calico," and he posed against the counter with his cigarette in his fingers.

BLANKET INDIANS

"You are kind and a friend," I lied, when I wanted to give him a shove that would ruin both his pose and his grin. "You see these Navajos are in no hurry. I can easily measure the calico for them and get the oranges and flour and candy."

He was perfectly agreeable but stayed all day, smoked our tobacco and told the customers I short-weighed the sugar. Then he'd say in English to me, "In Chin Lee, where I have been working in a store, we gave more sugar for fifty cents than you do. Shall I tell these Navajos to go to Chin Lee to get their sugar?" Thinking I did not understand, he had already told them just that, so all I could do was answer, "Of course, tell them. If sugar is so cheap in Chin Lee, I may go there myself to buy it."

When John at last went out, I heard the Old Lady whisper to her son, White Hat, "He lies; he lies very much."

To-Clazhin bent his head to speak confidentially to the Old Lady. "I have just come from Chin Lee. The trader there sells sugar for just what San Chee (meaning me) and her man sell it."

Even Mrs. Japon, John's mother, knew John for what he was. He might be her eldest son, but not her idol.

She had several young children of her own and was caring for a grandson and granddaughter whose parents were dead. All were lovely children. Since the men of her family were gamblers and the women poor weavers, there was never enough food or clothing. Mrs. Japon scolded every one at the top of her voice, but I did not blame her for saving her best efforts for John.

"*Yaa-de-la, olyea, she-zha-aad?*" (What do you call it, my female relative?), she shouted at me one day, as she came in the store door, her robe drawn tight about her and her hair uncombed. "The policeman wants my two beautiful grandchildren to go to the white man's school. They will make white folk of them, as they did of my oldest son; they will cut off their hair! They will make *moui chong-i* of them! All *deneh* who cut their hair are thieves. John is a thief. I have heard it said. All *deneh* say so."

Every one in the store listened. And they listened without smiling, both because the situation to them was serious and because they feared the old woman's tongue.

To be a coyote, "*moui*," was the last word in Navajo insult. They used *moui* for thief too, and to be called an ugly coyote was the worst possible.

"But how did Hosteen Be Dugi Yazzi know of your grandchildren, my mother?" I asked.

As well as the Navajos, I knew that Hosteen Be Dugi Yazzi, the Navajo policeman, had been in the neighborhood for several weeks, hunting children of school age.

"*Ai, ai.* It was that coyote, John, who brought him to my hogan. Without my knowing. He brought him. And the children playing before the hogan. *Ai, ai* —— "

John, in his white man's clothes and Navajo jewelry, had ridden up behind his mother and was making a show of tying his horse to a piñon tree, but every one within half a mile of Mrs. Japon's voice knew what she thought of school-trained Navajos and policeman.

BLANKET INDIANS

"Now that Hosteen Be Dugi Yazzi has seen the children, he will keep coming back," she told the world and John. "It was John who brought him. John went to the white man's school. One like John is enough. The children stay at the hogan."

The Indians were respectfully silent, but some answer was expected.

"Perhaps the children would be better off eating and living warm at the government school," I suggested. "They can't be worse coyotes than John is. They may be different. They ——"

"They better be different," she squealed and said it all over again.

The Indian agent, the highest official on the reservation, wanted one child in each family sent to the government school; but most families hid the children from the authorities. John Mitchell's white training had made him forget he was a Navajo, or else he had figured there would be more for him to eat if the children were in school.

After days of scolding and shouting Mrs. Japon told Be Dugi Yazzi she would let her grandchildren go to the school. "They will be warm and fed, warm and fed. But John is *moui chong-i*" (ugly coyote), she told me.

As heartily as I agreed with his mother that John was a coyote, I felt a kind of pity for John. He had been trained at the government school to be a mechanic; the white men did not want to employ him and the only machinery on the reservation was the scattered windmills from which John was as adept as any other Navajo at removing every detachable part. He would take

the policeman to his mother's hogan and sneer openly at
things sacred to his people, but there was something
furtive in the sneering — a hint of maybe-they're-right-
and-the-school-people-wrong feeling.

We were still discussing John and the policeman
when a messenger came, urging that I go at once to the
hogan where the Little Cranks were living temporarily.
Their little boy was sick.

In such a situation I feared my Navajo would not
be adequate and asked John to go with me.

They had been singing to the child for three days.
I found the hogan full of smoke and Indians.

The child was lying against his mother, who held him
in a sitting position. He was stark naked; his hair was
tousled and full of dirt and the herb leaves they had
used; his little body was too dirty for words, and on
the side where the swelling of the rupture was, the dirt
or "medicine" was caked deeper than on the rest of the
body; but he wore a string of beautiful turquoise. He
had a sheep pelt under him and a blanket to put over
him when he lay still enough; but he was delirious and
clawed his hair, waved his arms and threw the blanket
every direction.

The doctor or medicine man, Hosteen Untiligi, for
whose little boy I had shortened the sleeves of the coat,
sat at one side, facing the child. His medicine sticks
were spread on a piece of calico; in a turtle shell was a
little water with some powdered herb in it. He took a
medicine stick, dipped the end in the water, moistened
his lips and the child's, shut his eyes and took up the
song.

I did my best to learn a little of the song — the music, I mean — but could not remember a note of it. It was not loud, it had few notes. No one beat time, but there was accent and measure in the singing.

Two helpers shook rattles made of skin of some kind with feathers tied to wooden handles. In each rattle were two spotted beans. They had come to me the day before for the beans and had spent half an hour choosing them. The helpers' singing was not in unison with the doctor's but was a sort of whining accompaniment. They did not move their lips at all and I could not tell one voice from the other.

The end was so abrupt and unexpected and the final note so peculiar that the silence just hurt for a minute. I felt as if something might really happen, and it was evident that the Indians also waited; but there was nothing. After a long minute, in which John Mitchell was a Navajo with the others and waited with them, he looked at me and shrugged his shoulders.

After the moment of dead silence, every one motionless, the doctor dipped the tips of a bunch of eagle feathers in the ashes of the fire, which occupied the center of the hogan, and tapped twice on the boy's feet, on his knees, on the sore spot, on his shoulders and on his head. Then he stood over the boy, who was now lying down, and fanned the full length of his body back and forth, back and forth, as he sang. I was glad of the fanning, because it blew the ashes out of the child's face.

I had with me some flannel for hot packs, and while the singers rested, the mother heated water and I put them on. The singing began again as I worked, so I thought I was safe in keeping it up.

In spite of seeing me put on the hot packs and feed the child broth I had taken down, they did not want to do either, themselves. They cautioned me not to let the boy bite me. He did shut down on my little finger once and I had to pry his jaws open with the spoon.

On the way home I asked John, "Why does the little boy wear the beads?"

"Good medicine," he answered. "But it would not be for a white child?"

"No," and I wondered how to word a question that would make John explain exactly how the beads were good medicine.

Before I was ready he said, "They will be buried with the child."

I had guessed that.

John took my arm politely to help me over some rough ground.

"You whites take beads and baskets and even bodies from graves?"

"Only from old, old graves," I gasped and launched into a stumbling explanation of the work of an archæologist.

When I had finished, he nodded. "Would you take from an old, old grave?"

"Not here," I stammered, "but perhaps in a country a long, long way off — across the ocean, maybe."

I went alone over to that hogan twice a day for three days. All the time the child was growing weaker and weaker. The family moved out of the hogan and camped in a brush shelter with friends and relatives who came to comfort them; the father and three or four other men with the things for the grave waited in the hogan. The medicine man, saying there was no use to sing any more, left. On the fourth morning I met the child's grandfather before I reached the hogan. He was going to the family camp to tell them the boy was dead.

I went on and found the father and two men with the dead boy. The body was so covered I could not tell whether it had been dressed, but I knew the turquoise were to be buried with it.

The three men buried the body and burned the hogan. No one else, not even a member of the family, besides the father, was near.

Two days later in the afternoon the three men who buried the body came into the store looking exceedingly sober. They told Ken that some one had been near the grave. They had seen tracks, man tracks crossing the regular trail and going around the hill toward the foot of the bluff where the grave was.

Only the men who bury a body know the exact location of a grave. The family knows the general site selected and this information — no one knows just how — gradually becomes general among the Indians; but neither a member of the family nor any one else ever goes near a grave.

In this instance, no one had dared go see for himself if the grave had been disturbed, but the family stood ready to kill any one who had so much as looked for the exact spot. They asked Ken to follow the tracks and seemed satisfied when he said he would.

The next morning Ken went out and found the tracks were made by a man who was following a burro trail. The animal had crossed the road, wandered past the bluff where the grave was, and turned back to the road. When Ken got back to the store, the father, mother and other members of the family were there waiting; the mother almost in tears and insisting on holding my hand across the counter.

Upon asking Ken what he had found, the men were relieved to learn that the grave had not been touched but were angry and uneasy because some one had been near it. A man who was listening to the talk said that the father of a neighbor had come from Flagstaff on a visit and had lost a burro. He it was who had made the tracks; and, as he knew nothing whatever about the death or the grave, he could not be suspected.

On the instant the situation changed. The tension relaxed; every one drew a comfortable breath and they had a cigarette all around.

How even the men who buried a body could tell under which particular rock it was, was more than I could understand. They often buried at the foot of a bluff where there were heaps of loose rock and they exercised every precaution to make rocks and ground look undisturbed.

It was immediately after the death of the ruptured boy and the upheaval about the suspected grave robbery that John Mitchell asked for a job hauling wool out to the railroad and bringing back goods for the store. His ponies were in fairly good condition and Ken gave him a try.

He made good time on the first trip and every can of tomatoes and head "bandie" listed on the invoice was present in the load.

One day in the height of the wool season the heathen had come early and stayed late, as usual. All day I had trotted. Five steps behind the counter to get five cents' worth of candy, five steps back; five steps to get five cents' worth of cookies and five back, four trips for four packages of coffee and make change after each package was delivered — all four packages bought by the same customer.

About nine-thirty P.M. we drove the crowd out and made for bed. Ken was almost asleep, Betty was snoring, and I had reached the cold-cream stage when definitely, though faintly, I heard that blowy whistle a Navajo drives his horses with. He kept up a continual noise of shooing, whistling and "get up there" in English. I took it he thought the white man had discovered a language the horse understood. Anyhow, I heard the freighters coming — two four-horse teams from Gallup.

I screwed the lid back on the cold-cream jar; Ken got up and dressed. I put on a kimono and hunted frantically for strings with which to fasten up my stockings. The teams came to the platform in front of our door and unloaded. All the savages came in again and stood around and impeded traffic, as we carried flour, coffee, canned goods, oranges, tobacco, sugar, handkerchiefs for head bandies, and corduroy pants. I checked the load and tried to understand the remarks they made about my appearance. Almost midnight, coal-oil lamps, piles of freight, Navajos and the one woman present in a kimona and her hair in a pigtail.

Well, it was one-thirty before we got the store cleared again, and then I had to read my letters while we ate a lunch of cheese and soda pop.

The oil was almost burned out of the lamp, and it was flickering and smelling, when there was a scratching on the door — not a knock, but it was a sound made by a human.

We listened. Again the scratching.

Ken opened the door.

In the gusty night, with heavy clouds blowing across a half moon, he did not see at first the man flattened against the side of the house.

"Let me in." It was John Mitchell's voice. Ken opened the door wider and John closed it quickly behind him.

There wasn't much more light inside than out, but we guessed that the turquoise — a string of them — he held out were exceptionally fine ones.

My hand was on Ken's arm and I felt the muscles tighten. If the necklace had been a rattlesnake, I would not have been so uneasy.

Ken yawned. "No pawn to-night. To-morrow, maybe. We sleep now."

"No pawn," John whispered. "I won them at cards. I sell to you. You send out by me to the jewelry store in Gallup. Money — plenty — for us both."

"Not to-night," Ken said and urged the Indian toward the door.

"To-morrow I go again to Gallup," John stood stock-still.

"Our light is out. I cannot see what they are worth to-night."

As we fumbled our way to bed in the dark, I asked Ken what was wrong.

"He probably stole them and is trying to get them out of his hands before the owner catches him."

I remembered John's question about white men robbing graves and told Ken. "He may be that big a fool," Ken answered.

After a trip to Gallup, a freighter usually rested his horses a day or two before starting back; but John, with four fresh horses, probably his mother's, was at the door before we were up. Luckily, no one else was there, and Ken refused point-blank to have anything to do with the turquoise.

John hurried his loading and drove off.

A few days later strange Indians began coming to the store. They seemed friendly enough and traded some. Our own people were neither overfriendly nor hostile to them.

The strangers hung around three or four days and then one day did not appear. Ken said they were waiting for something and probably were not far away. I wondered if they were watching us but Ken said no.

When John Mitchell drove up with his load of freight, those fellows and a half dozen more that I had never seen before — all in war paint — rode to meet him. I saw them come down the hill past the well and I called to Ken. We both ran out on the loading platform.

They met Mitchell's wagon fifty yards from the store, circled about him and his team, singing a sort of chant. Then they all shot together. John's body sagged to one side and out of the wagon seat. His shirt caught on the brake and tore, and then the body fell in an awkward huddle to the ground. He had not made one move to save himself.

The strangers rode away.

The Indians in the store at the beginning of the fracas had watched with us from the platform. Now they were ready to go on with their trading.

Ken tried to persuade some of them to bury the body, but they refused. They wouldn't even go and drive John's team up to the store, but when Ken did that, some of them helped unload.

That night Ken and I buried John Mitchell. Even his mother did not appear.

We found out later that he had taken the turquoise from an old grave a long way from Covered Water. He was white man enough to do that; and, in the crisis, Indian enough to accept what his own people called just punishment.

VIII · LIFE AS USUAL

AFTER John's death, the busy wool-season routine seemed quiet and peaceful. Day after day Ken ran from cellar to corral, to flour tent, to wool tent, to store, and left me on duty behind the counter; and I liked it, even if my feet did hurt.

All the spring, after I had shortened the coat for Hosteen Untiligi's son, the heathen had urged me to sew for them. I did what I could. We were buying the farm and every half dollar helped. I had begun on a full-length red-plush coat for Untiligi before wool season began.

Every day he would push through his ilk, who were massed about the counter redeeming their pawn and trading with their wool money, to ask, "How soon?"

When most of the wool was in and the work slackened, Ken would still come crowding through my room with a bundle of wool as big as a mattress and say, "You'll have to go into the store. That heathen has seventeen dollars yet."

Another might have only seventeen cents, but I'd have to leave my sewing and tear calico, cut plug tobacco, scoop sugar, or toss a few twenty-five pound sacks of flour up on the shelf, where we could reach them easily.

But the plush coat did progress. It was gorgeous. Cherry red, lined with black sateen and reaching to the ankles. When my part of the work was finished, Untiligi put five buttons made of half dollars with an eye soldered on one side, down the front of the garment, seven made of dimes on each sleeve, one on each lapel and seven on the slit I had made up the back, so he could ride in the coat. The first day it was in his possession, he gambled, lost it and came right back and ordered another; but even so early as 1915 we were feeling the pressure of the war and were never able to get more of the red plush. He was broken-hearted for months from disappointment.

Friendship

It was after the death of the ruptured boy that the child's mother, Mrs. Little Crank, and I became fast friends — at least, that was her interpretation.

Ken had given her husband the name, Little Crank that first day, when he had raised such a rumpus because his beads were not to be found, and it stuck.

Navajos never mention their names except to old and tried friends. We therefore designated them by what we could remember of their features, manner, or whatever; and because our version was easier to spell and easier to say, we often kept it on the books after we learned the Navajo's real name.

Little Crank was a give-away of that gentleman's nature. His wife matched him in disposition. After the boy's death, they moved some fifteen miles from the store but rode back to trade, because they considered me their particular friend; that is, their claim on me was greater than the claim of those whose hogan I had not visited.

No Indian ever accepted at first the price — any price — we offered for a goat hide, blanket or whatnot, and we could not make them understand that our prices were determined by what we could get from the wholesaler. True to this principle, but more particularly because of this assumed old and tried friendship between Mrs. Little Crank and myself, she always asked for an extra half dollar on a seventy-five-cent goat hide.

Another good bit of business on her part was to give me a quarter for *sekissigie*. *Sekiss* means friend, and anything given for *sekissigie* or friendship is given as a flattering tribute. Mrs. Little Crank liked to have others see that we exchanged *sekissigie*. She came up to me, just as she did immediately after the boy's death, grasped my hand, leaned her head on my shoulder and after a long moment put the twenty-five-cent piece in my hand. "For *sekissigie*," she whispered. "Not to buy anything. I give to my mother, to my kind older sister. Oh, no, it is not to buy anything but because my sister, my older sister, is good and kind."

After that she stood around and waited for what I should give her. I tried her out on various things and she insisted on a full twenty-five cents' worth, or a little more. If I gave her a can of peaches worth twenty cents, she said, as she accepted it, "And some candy, five cents' worth of candy in a paper bag, and an orange, two oranges for the children." If I gave her a nickel's worth of stick candy, she said, "It is very little. There are not enough sticks in the bag."

Then she stood around another hour or two and whispered, "For *old, old* friendship give me two cans of peaches." Ken said we were not to allow ourselves to be wheedled out of too much, so I had to play I didn't hear her.

After the *sekissigie* exchange, Mrs. Little Crank did her buying; then she shook hands and promised to come again.

One day both Mr. and Mrs. Little Crank were trading out a forty-dollar beef that was in the corral to be butchered in the morning.

Forty dollars in silver makes an imposing pile, and those two stacked it up between them on the counter, that was high enough so they could just lean their elbows on it, put their heads together and whispered. Ken insisted, as he always did, that they pay something on the pawned beads and bracelets tied up in a calico rag. This I dug out from the pile of similar bundles under the counter; we untied the corners and spread out the array of white, coral and silver beads, slender silver bracelets that had a pawn value of one dollar, and heavy turquoise-set wristbands that were in for ten dollars or more.

At any time a Navajo may pass across the counter his bracelets, buttons, rings or a bridle — any and all hammered out of silver money — and demand trade for them. The beads are of silver, shell or coral; but all are valuable and they constitute the Indian's only collateral and the trader's greatest responsibility.

The Little Cranks had a big bunch in pawn for their winter's supplies.

"We will pay two dollars on the big bracelet," began the Little Crank, taking two silver dollars from the stack in front of him and placing them forward, as if he were playing checkers. "And one dollar on the white shell beads, and one dollar on the silver beads and fifty cents on the coral beads," and he put another pile out. I gave him fifty cents in change, while Ken changed the marks on the tickets fastened to each article and told them how much was left to be paid on each. At that there was a wail. "You said six dollars more on the white beads? My friend, you are wrong. You lie; there are five dollars only. My wife here remembers the time well; it was before the last full moon that we bought flour and sugar, a shirt and a silk handkerchief, and some candy. Five dollars was the amount and any one who says it was six, lies."

We waited quietly while Mrs. Little Crank took up the wail, "He says five dollars. It must be five dollars. Your paper lies. Put on a new tag that says five dollars and I will pay when I finish the next blanket. Those are good white beads; we like them."

Ken said, quite indifferently, "Yes, they are good white beads; that is why that other trader let you pawn them for ten dollars over a year ago. I think you should wear them again, because you forget them when they are here. See, I take six of the silver dollars and the beads are yours again. If you forget the price on any pawn, it is time you had it back at your hogan. See, now you have pretty white beads to wear home and your husband has none."

"But I do not want to take the beads to-day; I want the six dollars. I lied before; it was six dollars," admitted Mrs. Little Crank. "Let us have the six dollars."

"Why, certainly," said Ken, all willingness. "We make a new ticket. See — for six dollars. You have just pawned your white beads, my friend. Now what will you buy? Flour? Coffee? Here, take these six dollars and trade with them, then you can count the purchases easily," and he handed back the money and the Little Cranks traded happily on.

They were staying all night, to be on hand for the killing of that beef in the morning, and informed Ken they would take the beef's liver, intestines, and some fat back home with them. She said they were almost out of mutton fat at home and that they all liked their white dough fried in beef fat. It did not seem to occur to them that we had paid for all of that steer, inside and out. When Little Crank himself suggested that Ken give him seven dollars for the hide, Ken had to explain that when he paid for a steer in the corral that steer's liver, intestines and even the hide were included; but added that they could stay and find something at the butchering that they could take back.

That butchering in the morning was a quarrelsome affair on the part of the two Little Cranks; Ken hurried the business as much as possible in order to get rid of them.

The Little Bidoni

Such things as plush coats might buy white enamel pans for the farm kitchen I looked forward to, but it was the trade of the Utcity family that would be noticeable in buying the farm. When we went to the post, Mr. Taylor told us that that family alone would keep a small store going.

Utcity, an old man of much dignity and great power everywhere on the reservation, was the head of a really formidable group of sons and daughters, their wives and husbands and children.

The Little Bidoni, meaning little son-in-law, was the business head of the whole family, which lived in the high canyons and rough country of Black Mountain itself, where they were twenty miles from our store and forty miles from the one at Chin Lee.

The Little Bidoni had the biggest flock of sheep in the region. He married the three pretty daughters of old Hosteen Utcity, and each of them had a big flock of sheep. He paid for his wives with cattle, so he and his father-in-law owned a big herd of cattle; and he and his wives owned sheep and more sheep and more sheep.

He had not liked the last two traders who had managed our store and never so much as stopped to rest or to water his horses when he went by; but we were watching our chance to make a friend and a customer of him.

And then, after all our watching and waiting, we had to let the Little Bidoni drive by us and take his wool to Chin Lee. We saw him and his six-horse team and two wagons piled high with big wool-sacks drive by a quarter of a mile away. The road ran much nearer the store; but we had had no recent rain or snow and so, the ground being hard, he cut straight across the big bend that swung in to the store. He saved his team a mile or so of pulling and lost us our chance to get his wool that spring.

For half an hour Ken watched those two big loads crawl past. They dipped out of sight in the hills and later we saw them again on the sky line of our valley.

Losing that chance cut our profits for the year more than I cared to think. The farm seemed gone forever.

Ken didn't say a word.

But ten days later the Little Bidoni was ours. Whoever would have thought he had more wool than those two big loads he hauled all the way to Chin Lee? Again he came by, headed for Chin Lee, with two more such loads. The ground was wet and soft and he had to follow the road and swing in by the store.

To the north and west of us there was a deep wash, not steep on our side; but the opposite bank was the last slope of a rough hill. Of course, no road in that country was graded. As his teams came down the hill and made the sharp turn down into the wash, the wagons slid dangerously on the wet road, and the next minute a part of the topheavy load of wool rolled off. I was watching from the kitchen window and, expecting the next minute to see those six horses tangled up and struggling, I shouted to Ken and all the Indians in the store to run help, before the horses hurt themselves; but I could have saved my voice. They were all outside and on the way.

I learned later that Ken was on our side of the wash, warning the Little Bidoni before he started down the hill that the road was bad. He reached the heads of the lead horses as soon as the driver himself.

I watched our Indians run down the sandy slope that was our side of the wash, past the wells and climb the opposite side to where the narrow road wound among the trees and rock ledges. It was just there that Ken and the Little Bidoni were keeping the horses from wrecking everything.

How men do love to gather around a wreck and offer advice! I couldn't hear what was said; but Navajos are never quiet under such circumstances, and I could see that Ken and the Little Bidoni were talking together a little aside from the main group. In a few minutes all hands began to roll woolsacks out of the way and un-hitch the horses.

An Indian came tearing across to me with a note which read: "Make coffee. Open cans. Feed this outfit. Send back pick and two shovels." I sent the pick and shovels back by the bearer of the note, looked out the window again, counted the Indians and did as I was told.

Between frying meat, opening cans and making biscuits (there wasn't bread enough in the house to feed so many), I looked out of the window. There was Ken fixing the bad place in the road, actually building a piece of road so the Little Bidoni could haul his wool to Chin Lee. The meal cooked, I watched the crowd load the woolsacks on the wagon again. It was almost sundown now.

Ken asked them all over to the store to eat, in pay-ment of the help they had been in fixing the road. He had wanted that road fixed for some time. An Indian is always ready to eat a free meal, so in they all came and sat on the floor and smacked their lips over the biscuits with meat, the tomatoes and coffee.

They were all so happy and at home that it was pleasant to see. Some of those men, having been around the store all day, knew that I had made doughnuts in the morning. Now one called to me, "*A la hone,* my sister, my mother, my female relative! Bring us the round brown breads I saw you cooking in the hot fat this morning. We are your hungry children and you must feed us. See, we are all your small boys."

Who, I ask you, could refuse, when confronted with

142

nine grins, nine sets of perfect white teeth in·nine smooth brown faces, all full of good will? I brought out every doughnut — and they ate them all.

After the meal, the seven who were our Indians — I mean who lived near — rode off home. The Little Bidoni and his assistant were preparing to drive by moonlight in order to reach Chin Lee as soon as possible; but as darkness settled down, I noticed a cloud of sparks like that from a blast furnace coming out of the smoke hole of our camp hogan. Ken had offered that runt of an Indian feed for his horses for the night, and I had heard him add, "In the morning, when it is light, I will mend for you some of the harness that was broken when the wagons slid."

The next morning Ken was out before sunup. In a few minutes, the Little Bidoni having joined Ken, the two of them dragged some harness into the store, got out some leather and they both held and cut and riveted.

The Little Bidoni appreciated a good job. "That is very good, my friend," I heard him say. "That makes the strap strong."

And Ken answered, "Yes. Very strong. You have strong horses so you need strong harness."

"I have a strong horse you have not seen. He is a red horse and very quick on his feet."

"Let me see this red horse some time, my friend. Is he for sale?"

"No, I ride this horse. He is not broken to pull a wagon. Perhaps some day I shall hitch him to the wagon. He is very strong."

"You must have your harness very strong before you

143

drive this horse or he will break something and get away."

"That is true. You, my brother, have two good horses. I have seen them here."

"Yes, my horses are good, but they are not stallions, like your strong horse. They are only good to ride when I go to look for cattle."

I couldn't hear Teddy-Witte belittled, so I remarked that our horses could run very fast if they could not pull a great load.

"That reminds me, my friend," Ken said carelessly, "you have a heavy load and there is a bad hill to go down, when you go off the mesa. Some day I shall have that road fixed so teams may go up and down safely, but just now the rains have washed out one side of it. A wagon has a hard time to get down. If the load is heavy, a wheel is sometimes broken. You see, I do not use that road because my teams go to Lugontale and the road that way is good."

Little Bidoni pulled on a leather string with his teeth and laced the edge of a tug neatly. "You buy wool here, my friend?"

Ken nodded, as he measured the length of leather thong he needed.

"What do you pay?"

Ken made a hole with his awl and thrust the thong through as he answered, "Oh, yes. I have bought some wool; I pay the same as the traders at Chin Lee pay. If you want to save yourself and your horses the trip over that very bad road, why do you not sell your wool here?"

144

"My brother is kind. He has been very generous to me, but I have promised this load of wool to one of the traders at Chin Lee in payment of a debt. I must take it to him."

I could see that Ken's respect for the Navajo went sky-high.

"My friend, you are right. If you owe a debt to the Chin Lee trader, go there and pay. Is the debt so large that all this wool goes to pay? You must have pawned many fine beads, my friend."

"You have guessed. I have much pawn there — two hundred and fifty dollars it will take to bring home all of my women's silver goods."

By this time the mending was finished and Ken and his new friend were separating the harness and the scraps of leather, string and rivets.

"Listen, my little brother," Ken said. "Let me give you two hundred and fifty dollars in money. You take one of your horses and ride to Chin Lee to-day. Pay all your debt and bring back your women's silver goods. When you return, we will weigh your wool, and I will buy it of you. I am sure there is more than enough wool for the two hundred and fifty dollars.

"After that, with a rested team and this strong harness and your two wagons, you shall take a load of wool for me to Gallup and bring back the goods I shall write for on a paper. And listen, do a wise thing I will tell you, because we are brothers.

"You will have wool money and in Gallup you can buy things cheaper than any trader can sell them so far out here. The things I write for on the paper shall not overload your wagons; you can bring back both my load and your own. Is this not good?"

For a long time the little Navajo did not speak but sat studying Ken, as he hammered copper rivets into a breast strap he had decided was not strong enough.

"Besides," Ken went on, as if he did not feel the steady look bent on him, "besides, you get paid a dollar and a half for each hundred pounds of wool you take to Gallup for me and a dollar and a half more for each hundred pounds of goods you bring back. It is a good bargain. Your horses are strong, too."

"Years ago," said the Little Bidoni very slowly, "I hauled freight for a trading store. The white man lied to me about the weights of the things I hauled, and because of his lying I did not have the money that was due me. I have not hauled freight for any man since. I do not want to haul freight; there is too much to do at my hogans. I have seen you and worked with you while you helped me, and I will make one trip to Gallup to spend money for things we need in the hogans; but my women may want to go. I cannot start without first seeing them. This is their wool.

"Listen to my plan, my brother. I will take the two hundred and fifty dollars and ride to Chin Lee to-day. My cousin here will ride another horse to the hogans and tell the women what I do. Any that want to go to Gallup will come here and be ready, when I return from Chin Lee with the silver goods.

"If you say it is good, my cousin will bring from the hogans two more wagons and six more horses. We will load all the wool and hides you want to send out. My

146

women will have money for the wool we will sell you and I will have money for the loads I haul.

"We leave here to-morrow for Gallup and be back in seven days with the load you will order on paper. I know the places that load the freight wagons. Is it well?"

Ken held out his hand and they clasped solemnly. I brought out a canvas bag of money and they counted out two hundred and fifty dollars. Though silver has a meaning to Indians that paper money never has, Ken persuaded Little Bidoni to take all the banknotes we had, since it was lighter to carry and he was going to give it all to the Chin Lee trader. The silver jewelry would be heavy, so we gave the Navajo the canvas bag to bring it back in.

He rode off to Chin Lee; we began to make out our orders and I wrote letters half of the night, as we had sent out no mail for two weeks.

There was great hustle and running about the next day, when two of Little Bidoni's wives arrived in a nice top buggy. They were decked out in velvet, gorgeous Pendleton robes with white fringe and more jewelry than I had ever seen before on two women. I wondered what they would do with what their husband was bringing from Chin Lee, but that did not bother them. They put on bracelets, rings and necklaces until they clanked when they moved; and, because of the weight, must have been comfortable only when sitting still. Their wrists and fingers were stiff with rings and bracelets with turquoise settings.

Both of them wore shiny, new brown sateen skirts with enough other skirts under them to make the wearers move as if they were wearing hoops. One had on a black and the other a red velveteen shirt; these made the best of backgrounds for the bright necklaces. All the materials were the best carried by any trader.

On their feet were red-brown tanned moccasins, fastened with bright silver buttons; white-tanned buckskin wrapped their legs. This was the last word in luxury of dress. Very few Navajo women had the buckskins to use, but they all liked to wear such wrappings when riding horseback. Since these ladies were in full dress, they wore them even though they had come in a buggy.

They bought very few things in the store but were pleasant and nice; when they couldn't understand my accent, they patted me and laughed. I liked them and wanted a picture of them but didn't dare mention it or show a kodak.

The six-horse teams and the top buggy pulling away from the store were quite a sight. The women carried three hundred dollars in wool money, I knew. Ken declared he didn't care if he didn't make a dollar out of that particular deal. We were now friends with the Little Bidoni.

IX · LIFE UNUSUAL

THE first three months of butchering, the trade of
the Utcity family and the first wool season enabled us
to make a payment on the farm.

"Whoops, let's celebrate," I cried, as the Old Man
rode away toward Gallup, with that letter containing
a check for five hundred dollars in his pocket.

"How?" and Ken turned to enter the wool tent.

His lack of response hurt me. I hunted a job quickly.
For six weeks I'd been trying to get time to wash wool
for a comforter. It proved to be the sort of thing to
take my mind off intangible troubles. I used a barrel
of water, half a can of lye and two bars of soap.

I tried to run the wool through the wringer and
managed to get it unwound in something over two

hours. To dry it, I hung it in thin muslin sacks on the clothesline; but after a day in the Arizona sun and wind it was still wet, and I had to spread it over the warming oven on the range.

San Stosi, one of the young ladies of the neighborhood, worked carding it while I kept what she was not operating on draped over the oven door. She seemed delighted with the nice clean wool while I was chagrined at the sand and ticks she carded out.

While she worked, the girl sat on the floor — comfortably. That's a thing I never could do. I counted the edges of six skirts she had on but thought she wore only one shirt, a gray velveteen. Her beads were red coral and the buttons on the shirt were half dollars with eyes soldered on them. Tied to the fringe of her belt were strings of common white buttons, several strings of shells, some safety pins and a string of what I at last made out to be copper rivets out of overalls. Her hair was dark brown and very fine.

The Storm God

The hot weather crept upon us during April, but hit us with a boom early in May. At the end of one of the first blistering days, Japon Begay, Japon's sixteen-year old son who was cutting wood for my stove, called to us to come see the storm.

At the store the sun was shining and a gusty wind was blowing; but a mile and a half away was a cyclone. We could see the great, gray streaks of it and the whirling black column lifting the dirt and sand from the bluffs as it passed over. The dirt was drawn up the side of the bluff, across the top and into the air. It looked like a waterfall falling up. As the storm crossed a valley, it was almost red, and then it spread out into a great, black, smoky-looking top that tumbled and rolled within itself.

As we watched, the whole column disappeared over a mesa. A few large, splashing drops of rain fell at the store, with the sun shining at the same time.

We knew there were a few hogans in the path of the cyclone and perhaps there were flocks of sheep. Had we been in its path, that poor shell of a building would not long have been on the map.

It was really a wonderful sight. I had seen sand storms and rough breakers and blizzards, but this cyclone was by far the most exciting.

For days after the storm, it, or perhaps I should say he, was the main topic of conversation. We learned that a god traveled in such storms — a god who could see where he was going and who did everything intentionally.

What we would call a special prayer meeting lasting five nights had to be held for two little boys who were caught in the path of the cyclone with their sheep. The first, a lad of thirteen, on seeing and hearing the *neol-so* (big wind), tried desperately to drive his sheep to shelter. He crowded them until they jumped over a low bluff and then, without time to save himself, the boy threw his arms around a small tree. At that instant the wind struck him, took his feet from under him and whirled his body round and round the tree. His sheep dog was carried into the air and dropped unhurt among the sheep huddled at the foot of the bluff.

Hosteen Atothy Yazzi, Little Wind Doctor, the boy's grandfather, was a medicine man and was one of those officiating at the five-day ceremony.

The other boy, a younger lad, and one from Hosteen To-Clazhin's hogan, lived about five miles from the first. When the wind came, he dug with his hands around an old stump until he could get a grip on some of the strong roots. His family, who were several yards away, saw his feet waving in the air an instant before the cloud of dirt blotted out everything. After the storm passed, the boy was still alive, but not much more than alive.

Little Crank brought us a wagonload of corn that he had buried. Only the family knew where the grain was; but the god in the storm knew, and he found the corn and uncovered it. Now, since the god had touched it, it couldn't be eaten by people or fed to stock. Little Crank warned us not to eat it and made us promise not to sell it in the store or feed it to the horses. He said we could feed it to the chickens.

According to his own story, Blue Goat saved the store. He saw the wind coming and hurried out to change its course. He told us about it, with the gestures of throwing kisses with both hands and making pushing motions with outstretched arms. The fact that the storm was coming directly toward the store and turned and went by a mile and a half away proved his story.

Those nearer the storm than we were reported that stones and trees were flying, acres of dirt were in the air, and sheep and lambs went sailing skyward, to fall dead or nearly so at the edge of the wind. On the mountainside big spruce and pines were uprooted and thrown to the ground. Many Navajos saw in the black, tumbling cloud the god with the lightning shooting from his hands and two streams of it from the crown of his head.

I asked the Old Man who the god was, and he told me the story, prefacing it with the remark, "I cannot tell you all; you will not know the words."

It seemed that a sort of supreme god, Natoni, lived in the sky, "the same place Jesus does." Other gods were directed by him, and one of these came to the earth once in a man's lifetime to take back sheep, goats, ponies, *deneh* (people) for Natoni to use as patterns in his future creations.

It was this god who came in the storm. Every one understood that it was he who made the grass grow tall, brought lambs to the flocks and babies to the hogans. After his visit a good year was anticipated. Lots of grass meant fat sheep and big crops of corn.

It had been thirty years since the last visit of this god. The Little Wind Doctor, who had seen that other wind, sang the principal part in the five-night prayers for the two boys. The idea of the prayers was to ask Natoni not to take the boys for patterns or for company in the sky. This prayer seemed to change the Black God's mind, for both boys recovered from their bruises and lived.

An idea of self-protection was evidenced by the fact that for four days no Navajo went across the path of the cyclone without first putting some little black and white and red beads on the broken ground where the wind had been.

It rained and snowed for days after the cyclone. Each day we thought no one would come to the store; they would surely all stay home by the fire. But no. They seemed to gather to talk over the storm. Each went through the whole scene as he saw it.

We Plan to Build

It did not require a cyclone to convince Ken and me that the shack we called the Covered Water store was even more uncomfortable in summer than in winter. When Ken first bought the store, Mr. Taylor tried to keep me at Lugontale until a house suitable for a woman could be built. He said it was impossible for a woman to live in that shack.

Though Ken and I never talked the matter over, we knew, after he had spent two weeks at the store with Wolfer, we would work together in that shack until something better could be built.

When all through the spring and early summer the hot, dry wind sifted sand through more cracks than we knew existed even when a blizzard held the shack in its grip, we talked again with Mr. Taylor about a new building, and he agreed that we should hire Navajos to cut and haul the logs.

When Hosteen Utcity Betsilly Nez, Hosteen Utcity's brother, had been working at that job for three or four weeks, Ken sent me to see if the logs were at least as long as our wood-cutter's name and straight enough for roof rafters and floor joists.

Ken could look at a mountain five or fifty miles away and take the shortest route to a given point on the mountain and return. I couldn't do that. After a very few miles, all the hills and gullys looked alike to me; even the ones I had crossed I didn't recognize when I saw them in reverse, as one does on the return trip. Because of this, to Ken, incomprehensible failing of mine, White Hat went with me as guide.

We crossed the path of the cyclone and saw some of the uprooted trees; their trunks were splintered and the ground was covered with broken and scattered boughs. White Hat said the Indians would not burn the wood, even though it was cut, and wood cutting and hauling were slow and laborious processes for them.

So much for a tabu. I wondered if I had any such belief which kept me from using something I might as well have had. I couldn't think of anything available there that we didn't use — unless it was prairie dogs. The Indians assured us they were better than rabbit. They were vegetarians — the prairie dogs, not the Indians — but who wants to eat a dog?

Beyond the path of the storm we climbed an abrupt hill, the ponies making their way through rocks and brush. From the top we looked out over a wide valley, grass-covered, for there had been plenty of rain. Halfway across the valley we came to a fenced cornfield and a hogan and stopped for a drink. The woman who brought me a little bowl of water with her thumb in it was Mrs. Little Crank. Of course, she said her husband and family had moved their home after the ruptured child died. She shook hands, called me her sister and asked if I had brought her *"sekissigie"* (friendship).

A little farther on we passed an old man who called me his mother. After another hour of rocks and sun, a whoop from behind stopped us, and Dugi Begay loped up to ask where we were going. He pointed out a trail we had missed and rode on.

In another five or six miles we turned into a canyon where the rocky hillsides were one tumbled mass of stone, with here and there a scrubby tree. The floor of the canyon was barely wide enough for the road, made entirely by Navajo wagons. It alone gave evidence that any one had passed that way since Adam's time. Once we passed some mound ruins, but look as I would, I could see no masonry work in the rim rock to indicate cliff dwellings.

Big pines suggested a possible end to our journey, but it was another two miles before I saw the first pile of peeled logs. They were too small and I began to think the new store would not be built soon. We saw a second pile, only eight, but better logs, and there encouragement ceased. We rode miles and turned into another canyon where there was only a trail; all the time we looked to either side for the bright peeled logs that showed so plainly against the rocks and brush.

Instead, we saw a saddled horse. Leaving ours tied in the same place, we climbed the hillside and found Utcity Betsilly Nez trimming a felled tree — a big one. That short climb and what I had seen of the country

convinced me that I was not the person to hunt and
measure each log. I was too short-winded for mountain
climbing on my own legs. It was after noon too, and
I was perfectly helpless when my stomach was empty.
White Hat asked the man if we could go home with
him and get something to eat and water the ponies.

We could, and he rode ahead to tell his wife to cook
something. We jogged along, White Hat entertain-
ing me by telling me how he had once ridden two days
without a bite to eat. He laughed at me, but that did
not keep things from turning black around me. Those
miles before we rode up to the fenced-in water hole
were the longest in Arizona.

How it did help to see the ponies drink and to smell
something cooking at the summer hogan of cedar
boughs!

We tried to ride the ponies up to a wagon to tie
them, but such a barking, growling and uproar as the
nine dogs that had been asleep under it, did make! One
meant all he said, so I gave my horse to White Hat and
made my way to the hogan afoot.

How good the shade was! And there were blankets
and pelts at one side to sit on. The man of the house
was reclining on one pile. His wife sat between the fire
and some boxes containing cooking utensils. She was
peeling potatoes. Her married daughters sat beside her,
one peeling potatoes and one cutting up meat — a
fresh-killed lamb, I think. There were five younger
children and about fifteen hundred sheep and goats, the
former inside, and the flock barely outside, but held to
windward by two more children.

I lay down and thought that if it were not for the smoke, I could sleep. When I opened my eyes, the meat and potatoes were cut up together and boiling in a big frying pan. The bread, fried to a lovely brown, was piled in disks on a plate; a goat was trying to climb the outside of the hogan after the green on the cedar brush.

We ate. The tea was good; the mutton and potatoes were not what one would call tender, but the broth around them was fine; and I could have enjoyed raw-hide; the bread was all it promised to be, though there was no salt in it. Three of us ate from one bowl of stew; each had his own spoon.

As soon as I felt normal, we started slowly home and reached the store without seeing any one. Ken had some grape juice mixed with pleasant proportions of cold rain water and sugar. At half-past nine, though I had been sitting at the table in my nightdress and with my feet in cold water, I was only beginning to feel comfortably cool and sleepy.

A "Borning"

The Navajos held that the god in the cyclone would bring many sheep and ponies to the herds and babies in the hogans; I held the heathen themselves — the men — responsible for more than their god had on his mind.

I could not enough admire the strength and fortitude of the women. Within a week after her confinement, I would expect to be making custards for a white woman, but in that time Mrs. White Hat had almost finished a blanket.

LIFE UNUSUAL

Mr. and Mrs. White Hat lived about a quarter of a mile up the wash from the store. Every day the lady carried a keg of water slung on her back by a brow-strap and a pailful in her hand from our well to her hogan. She did this even the day before the baby came. The trail was sandy and hilly.

Up to the morning of her confinement she worked on a blanket. White Hat was not in the least concerned, though the death of his sister in childbirth the previous winter had plunged the family into grief too genuine to doubt. A death among these people meant both sacrifice and grief; every one gave much-needed robes, saddles, jewelry or something of the sort to be buried with the body. White Hat had given a new bridle and a silver belt. Such experiences did not make him more considerate, however, when the next new member of the family was expected.

Once, when Mrs. White Hat had washed a lot of wool and carried water, he kept a horse up so he could ride quickly to call the Navajo medicine man, should her pains turn out to be the final signs. Next morning, however, Mrs. White Hat was better and washed wool while White Hat went to a rabbit chase. He was gone all day and all night. There was horse racing after the rabbit chase. A crowd of thirty or more of the sportsmen came to the store on tired, sweaty ponies that had not had a drink or a bite to eat since noon the day before. There was a great demand for canned tomatoes and soda crackers. These were eaten in three minutes, and then there was a cloud of dust, as the tired ponies were whipped into a run over the hill and out of sight.

And Ken had to listen to another lecture from me on Navajo morals.

A few mornings after that we heard that the Navajos were gathering at White Hat's house for the "borning," Soon White Hat came dashing up on a dripping pony. As pale as a brown man could be, he came into my room instead of going to the store. I was sitting at the sewing machine. As I reached for the bottle of antiseptic with one hand and clean towels with the other, I wondered if I would be able to ride a horse without putting on riding clothes. How long would it take me to walk in the soft sand?

White Hat asked for tobacco. The medicine man wanted to smoke. After he got that, he said his wife had been sick a long time. Then he suggested that I go up to the hogan. I started, but he bolted by me on the trail before I was fairly on my way. Every Navajo at the store followed. I was so displeased I almost turned back, but the thought of Mrs. White Hat and my own inborn mania for the unknown kept me going on that sandy trail, hatless in the burning sun. It was July and really hot.

As I approached the hogan, I counted sixteen ponies standing around and saw a group of men in the summer hogan. A little flock of sheep and goats was being held against the rocky bluff and White Hat was just swinging a rope to catch one. I could hear the chant of the medicine man inside the main hogan, so I drew aside the blanket that hung over the doorway and went in.

That first glimpse will stay in my memory forever.

LIFE UNUSUAL

In all my imaginings of the crude Indian way of treating sickness, I had never once thought of such a thing as I saw. The hogan was cleared of everything. The ashes in the center of the floor were cold. Six women and three men, all the place would hold, were there. Mrs. White Hat fully dressed, knelt facing the east. With both hands she clung to a wool rope that was passed over a roof rafter and tied in a knot for her to grip. Behind her, with both arms clasped tightly around her body, was a man; the sweat poured from his face as he pressed it against her shoulder. Two women held their hands over Mrs. White Hat's on the rope; their faces were wet and drawn. A medicine man stood at her side, singing and tapping Mrs. White Hat on the head, shoulders and stomach with a bunch of eagle feathers.

Her hair was tumbled all over her head and face by his beatings; her eyes were an agony of pain; the lines of her face were deep; the sweat had dripped on the front of her red velvet shirt until it was thoroughly wet.

The man kneeling behind the patient spoke, and one of the other men took his place, putting his arms around her before the first withdrew his. With one hand he clasped the other wrist and put all his strength into the grip around her body; Mrs. White Hat leaned her head on her hands and groaned. When the pains came, the man had help from the others. They took hold wherever they could squeeze or press. They all talked at once and the medicine man sang high and fast and beat her with the eagle feathers wherever he could get in a tap. Mrs. White Hat clung to the rope, never once letting go, never lying down.

As the pains stopped, the man who knelt behind the patient rose and retired to the wall to sit down. The medicine man smoked a cigarette. The women wiped the sweat from Mrs. White Hat's face and held water to her lips.

At last, in the midst of some of this agony, the baby came. A woman who knelt in front of Mrs. White Hat on the sheepskin put her hands beneath Mrs. White Hat's skirt and brought out the child. She laid it down on the sheepskin with its head touching the sand of the floor. The bright direct rays of the sun from the smoke hole in the roof struck it squarely.

The men rose and joined the crowd outside. White Hat came in and looked at his wife but did not go to her. One of the women went out and came in with a pail of water; another held out the child as you might a jack rabbit, and the first took a cup in one hand, the pail in the other and threw water over the baby, as it was turned round and round and over. The water was cold; I felt of the pail to be sure.

I held one of my clean towels ready, but some one reached out with a dirty flour sack and would have wrapped the child in that, if I hadn't thrust the towel in where it would do the most good. They gave the child to me then. It was as cold as a wet beefsteak.

While I sat holding the newest member of the family, the next older child, a little boy about two and a half, was brought in. His one garment, a little black velvet shirt, was stripped off over his head; he cried and called to his mother, but for once she did not answer him. They took the little boy out in front of the hogan and emptied the whole pail of cold water over him. The crowd outside laughed and roared and told him he was a man now and no longer a baby.

Mrs. White Hat by that time was looking almost as usual. She drank some corn-meal gruel and talked a little with the women. They all seemed to be relaxed and were inclined to be gay and sociable. I was included in the fun and was urged to treat the whole crowd to candy.

Being unable to get the baby's feet warm, I passed it over to its grandmother, the Old Lady. She shook out a little lambskin, and, wrapping the baby in a dry towel, folded the skin across it and turned up the foot. This she tied firmly, and then made a roll of another sheepskin and laid the baby against it. Some one had a twisted wire ready and this was put over the baby, and a piece of muslin, which I had taken up, thinking of bandages, was thrown over the wire and the baby. The wire kept the muslin away from the baby's face. It went straight to sleep.

I got up to go. They all asked me to make lots of clothes for the baby. Outside a fire was burning and a young kid was boiling in a big pail. A woman was making bread, frying the dough in a Dutch oven, full of hot grease. Every one was happy in the anticipation of a square meal.

I went back through the hot sun and deep sand. How any Indian woman escaped blood poisoning I could not see.

Bear! Bear! Bear!

Early, very early before daylight one day in September Hosteen Cla pounded on our door, shouting, *"Shosh, shosh* (Bears, bears). Whiteman, come quickly; there is a bear among us." He was so plainly excited that even though Ken thought he knew there were no bears in this section and had been none for forty years, he dressed and went out, with me following, of course. How we laughed at the Indian's excited story.

At his house the women and children were making an early start to get a load of hay — the wild grass they cut with a knife and tie in bundles. A team of burros was hitched to the wagon; the children were about to climb in and the women were standing near when over the very hill against which the hogan was built a bear appeared, running straight toward burros, women and children.

The burros, those beasts that had not stepped out of a slow walk for six years, ran away, taking the wagon, or what was left of it after it hit a few rocks, with them; the women and children reached the hogan in nothing flat, but once inside had only a blanket with which to barricade the door.

The bear passed the corral where the sheep were and they broke out and scattered over most of Arizona, if we could believe the Indian's story. Cla, afoot, hurried to the store for the white man and guns. They had revolvers but no ammunition.

Ken tried to make Cla believe that in the half-light of dawn he had mistaken a yearling calf for a bear, but the fellow was so sure of his bear that at last Ken saddled Teddy, took the Winchester 30-30 rifle and, with the Indian running ahead, actually did find a bear's trail.

During the morning several Indians came into the store but tarried only briefly. A great hunt was on. Horseback and afoot, some ten men were trailing the bear up and down among the choppy foothills. Every one knew that in time the hunters would walk the bear down and catch up with it. This they were prepared to do, but they were anxious that Ken should be there with the gun when they overtook the animal.

It was noon when the Indians, who had gathered at the store, and I heard two quick shots from the 30-30. They echoed, so we couldn't tell how far away the shooting was; but in a short time the party appeared on the steep trail, the bear hanging across a horse.

Curious as the Navajos were, not for anything would one have gone close enough to touch that bear.

Hosteen Atothy Yazzi, Little Wind Doctor, came up to me and asked me to get for him, when Ken should dress the bear, the gall bladder. I promised and told Ken to cut it out whole and complete; then I found a tomato can for the old man to carry it home in.

Strong medicine. And difficult to come at. If our own medical men wanted bear gall, instead of being satisfied with ox gall, they would not get a supply much oftener than old Hosteen Atothy Yazzi did.

Blue Goat, Untiligi and even Utcity came up to me in the days that followed and indignantly demanded why I had given *all* the gall to one man; any one of them would have paid ten or twenty dollars for a part of that bear's gall. I had no idea they valued it so and promised them the gall from the first beef we should kill. They answered with a pitying grunt and stalked away.

"Cattle! No! Bear!"

The bear was fat and dressed well. We ate some of the meat but could not persuade the poorest of the Indians to touch it. Hosteen Cla and two brothers, men of forty odd, heavy and greasy-looking, had come to the store rather infrequently for months. The mother of the three had a sharp, savage, hook-nosed old face that made Ken name her the Old Buzzard. They lived over near Saluni but just before the bear incident had moved close to our store.

The Old Buzzard's first neighborly act was to steal a cooking pan of mine that was on a box by the back door; and the second was to ask me for the lid, because the ashes, she said, fell into the pot.

I said she should bring me the pan again.

"No, my daughter," she answered. "You have others, so you will give me the lid, and I will know you are your grandmother's friend." Thereupon she unrolled from her blanket wrap a clay jar, round-bottomed, deep and black. I gave her the lid for it and we were both happy.

It was shortly after the bear hunt that a ten-pound lard pail half full of bear's fat disappeared from a limb of the piñon tree that grew at the back door. When we checked off our callers, we decided that the Old

Buzzard, thinking the fat was lard, had taken it, pail and all.

Ken waited until the old woman made one of a crowd in the store and remarked casually, "The coyotes are bad here. One has come to the very house and taken the last of the bear fat."

Interest was at once intense and universal. Some one started to ask if the fat would kill a coyote but was interrupted by a wail of rage. The Old Buzzard leaned across the counter and called me everything in the Navajo calendar, for putting that pail out in the tree. She was so wild that finally the other Indians stopped laughing and began to look anxious.

She swore that all her family would get sick and die and it was my fault.

When she stopped for breath, I told her we had eaten the bear fat and liked it. It hadn't killed us; neither would it kill her. She only screamed and began, as nearly as I could make out, telling me about my ancestry.

I told her I'd give her some medicine to protect her family from harm. That calmed her down, and when I gave her an aspirin tablet for each one in her hogan, she went home to give it to them quickly and save their lives.

Still, even after we heard that men with dogs had killed eleven bears in the Lukachukai Mountains, the Indians insisted that our bear had come for no good; they still expected disaster, and according to their idea it came, months later.

DESERT WIFE

A Dance

The early part of October, 1915, was marked only by never-ceasing wind. Sand sifted through every crack and there were plenty of them in that shell of a building. At last I refused to clean anything and spent spare moments studying the plans for the new store building, with rooms attached. Could we possibly be moved in another year?

Unexpectedly the wind lessened and, wonder of wonders in a place like Covered Water, a friend came to visit me. She was a real tenderfoot. Everything in Arizona was new and strange to her — the Navajos newest and strangest.

One evening the Old Man came to the store to get a load of canned goods, crackers and tobacco to sell to a crowd at a dance, — a social, not a ceremonial dance.

Polly nudged me. "Could we go?"

I asked Ken.

"You'll wish you hadn't," he grunted, "but go with the Old Man if you don't know any better."

We didn't.

We dressed for the occasion in Stetson hats and Pendleton robes. Navajos do not wear their own blankets, as they are not pliable enough to wrap closely.

That ride! Four miles of sand and brush. Our driver flapping the reins and yelling at every step and the little ponies fairly digging in their toes! They had to run on the down grades because the Old Man never put on the brake. Once we got out and walked — minus our robes

168

— and helped push the wagon out of a deep, sandy wash.

A mile from the gathering we could hear singing, then we smelled piñon smoke and soon could see the fires. As we climbed a rise, we saw against the full moon, horizon high, the singers standing in a tight group, heads bent together; the horses and wagons were dark masses beyond the fires. The Indians were all over the place.

Our wagon, stopped at the edge of the crowd, made a grand-stand seat.

In the center of the group of singers was a drummer. The song was in unison and the rhythm perfect, though the drum beat each note rather than the time. The singers swayed a little as they sang. The crowd was very quiet; no one spoke loudly; now and again a man came softly to the wagon, bought a can of tomatoes and a box of crackers and melted into the crowd; meat was cooking over the scattered fires. As our eyes became accustomed to the light, we realized that what we had thought to be a heap of saddles and bridles, blankets, etc., was sleeping Indians. Each was wrapped in a robe, and some fifteen of them were lying like pups in a basket, men and women.

The crowd was mostly men, the majority strangers to me. Several came to the wagon to give us the "once over" and shake hands. One spoke very good English, and we learned that this was the last night but one of the dance. It had started a week before, about one hundred and fifty miles away. The singers and a few followers were permanent, composed the troupe, as it were, but the others were local and new every night. There were some five or six hundred in the audience, for it was an audience, so far.

About midnight, the everlasting singing becoming tiresome, we wanted to go home. The moon was very bright now, but we did not dare walk, because of wild cattle. We asked for horses; but they did not want to send any one to bring the ponies back and we had to stay. One of our Indians got robes and spread them under the wagon on the ground; and, wrapped in our own robes, we crawled under. We left orders that we were to be wakened when the dancing began.

Laugh! Imagine how silly two lone white women felt! Under a wagon and in a bunch of savages! When any one came to the side of the wagon to buy something, we could hear the Old Man say, "The white women are under the wagon." The newcomer would stoop down, look under and say, "*A-la-honi.*" (Well, I'll be darned; or, For goodness' sake!)

Suddenly, just as we had dropped to sleep — fancy sleeping — the wagon began to roll backwards, horses were kicking and snorting and the dust was thick under the wagon. We both left that place on all fours, Polly out one side and I out the other, into threshing horses and yelling Indians. Some one grabbed me by the arm and picked up my trailing robe. How they ever kept their shawls on, I didn't see. Mine dragged all the time.

The uproar stopped. Since the singing seemed to be going on just the same, we crawled back under the wagon; but in the mix-up a bottle of soda pop had been broken on my side of the bed and I got into it and the broken glass. Of course, we couldn't sleep again, and soon they told us the dance was about to begin.

The singers changed their stand to the edge of the dancing space, opposite a big fire. The old fellow with the drum came forward and did a solo. Another fellow stood up and talked at length about a stolen bridle and saddle. Every one listened respectfully, but no one answered. The singers gathered about the drummer and sang another tune, and then the dance began.

Did I say dance? That would seem to imply fun. But of all the tired, uninterested people, those men were the worst I ever saw. We stood up to see better and thanked fate we hadn't been able to go home when we wanted to.

The girls in their very "best" clothes walked solemnly up to the ring of onlookers, seized a man by the coat or robe and pulled him, protesting, to the clearing, if he did not get away by might and main. Once in the open, the man ceased to struggle and stood quiet. The girl, still holding to the back of his robe, started around him backward on her tiptoes, lightly. The man turned slowly round and round, all the time looking bored to death. There was not a laugh, not a smile, not even a willingness in the whole performance. It was unspeakably funny to Polly and myself.

The greatest joke of the evening was that one of the girls mistook me for a man and got hold of my robe and nearly dragged me out before she realized who I was. My resistance, of course, was part of the game; and the girls never looked up to see who their victim was. One or two men standing near laughed a little, but the girl did not change expression; she merely reached for another partner.

The man has to pay the girl ten cents, more or less, for each dance. One fellow came to me to pawn his wrist guard for fifty cents, because the girl was holding his hat until he paid up. I had only a dollar with me, and it was only a few minutes before some one needed the other fifty cents.

They danced until about three and then the singers began again. Polly curled up on the wagon seat and I found a place among some boxes in the back. We had a short nap before daylight but were glad when the Indians began to hitch up. They sang until sunup, so we drove off and left them singing.

We were hungry and glad we came and glad we were going home, but about a mile out three horsemen came dashing up behind; the Old Man stopped. They talked a minute and then we were asked to take two horses and ride to the store. The wagon was to go to the stand for the next night.

Calamity! We had on narrow skirts. I couldn't speak enough of anything but store talk to do much good. All I could say was that we couldn't ride because we had no pants. Laugh! Those fool Indians almost killed themselves. But as there was nothing to do but ride, we got on the horses, put our robes over our laps to hang down each side, and with our shadows long before the rising sun, we strung out behind our escort and loped the three miles in to the store without a break. We got home in time for breakfast.

Um-m, yes, we disposed of a few graybacks first, and

Ken did not for a minute let us forget we brought some home.

Kismas

Before the birth of Mrs. White Hat's baby, more frequently while the wind blew in October and without ceasing, after that dance Polly and I attended, the heathen asked, "How long 'till Kismas?"

Christmas to us meant warm fires, red berries, gifts in tissue paper. We found that the Navajo "Kismas" included the warm fires, but everything else was novel enough to make history.

We planned to watch the benighted Navajo cook dinner; we had even declared we would eat with them; we would spend the day watching their games. For our treat we prepared a hundred small bags each containing candy, cookies and a red apple.

Christmas Eve the heathen began to arrive over these hills. There were wagonloads of women and children and scores of men and young people on horses. Everybody was dressed in his best: beads, bracelets and silver belts glistened against the bright-colored velvet shirts and glossy sateen skirts, with miles and miles of flounces. I had made several of the skirts and I knew how many miles long a flounce was.

By dark some two hundred Navajos were present. The Utcitys were there: the head of the house in all his dignity, the Little Bidoni and his three wives, soft-spoken and sweet, and all the other sons and daughters and husbands and wives; the Little Cranks, living up to their name; the Old Lady and Old Man, with their children and grandchildren; Robert, greeting old friends, and White Hat and Mrs. White Hat and the children; Japon and his wife and their progeny, Mrs. Japon and the Old Lady giving each other a wide berth. Cla was present with his brothers and the Old Buzzard. Everybody's friends were present and all their relatives.

Apparently they expected "Kismas" to begin at once. Expecting to supply meat for the Christmas dinner, Ken had killed a beef, but now he took down a hind quarter and cut steaks and more steaks until there was enough to go around. The adults came and took what they needed for their families for supper and for breakfast on Christmas morning. What they did not eat at once they were afraid to put down because some one would steal it, so all the evening they strolled about with great raw beefsteaks in their hands. Mrs. Japon and the Old Buzzard each had two.

We had provided several loads of wood so they could help themselves; and the Christmas fires, big and little, were all over the place. They were so all over the place, we were uneasy. One family settled down and built their fire within two feet of the walls of that frame shack of a store building. Ken had to go out and insist that they move elsewhere. They were indignant and thought it quite fussy in me to go out and shovel dirt over the bed of live coals they left.

Big fires were built on the level space, where the dancing was to be, and these, added to the light of a full moon, made the night so bright we could see the whole landscape around. The dancing was just for the Indians' amusement and ours and was in no sense ceremonial.

Christmas Eve the heathen began to arrive over these hills

Now and then some of them danced a figure from a ceremonial dance but without the costumes and other accessories. The music was made on a clay water jar with water in it and a rawhide stretched over the top. One fellow played this, or beat it, and others shook rattles made of paper bags with beans in them.

The best dance of the lot was one performed by some of the older men. They had to dance and sing because the younger men knew neither the proper songs nor the dance; and Utcity, the Singer, and the other six who made up the figures sang, laughed and kept up the most violent sort of exercises until they dropped panting to the ground. They all assured us that when they were young men they could keep it up all night, but now they were old and full of meat besides, and they couldn't do what they used to do.

With that dance and others, and wrestling and racing about the fires, there was plenty of activity. There was nothing cold or solemn about the gathering; every one was laughing and happy. They were a most fun-loving people and laughed at the same things we thought funny.

All the evening I was trying to bake two loaves of fruit cake. It was done when we finally went to bed at midnight — done with a thick crust an inch deep all over it and a core of good cake in the middle. Keeping an oven fire of pitch wood and watching the dancing outside had been too much for the success of the cake. The wood-burning stove was temperamental at its best.

All night we smelled the piñon smoke from the camp fires, and when a different smoke drifted into our window, we got up and followed it to find that some one had put box boards on his fire. Lady Betty was nervous and growled every time we or any one else moved. When we got back in bed, after tracing the source of non-piñon smoke, she came to the side of the bed and put her cold nose in my hand. After a little she lay down with a loud sigh, but got up at once if she could not feel my hand. My arm was numb from keeping the hand where she could reach it. Poor Betty! She didn't get much sleep that night and a hard day she had ahead of her, too. Wild reservation life was no joy to a blooded bulldog like Betty.

What with our uneasiness about the Indian fires and their early rising habits, we were up early Christmas morning. While the men and boys went out to the flat mesa to race their horses, we women folk thought about dinner for the crowd. By eleven o'clock Mrs. White Hat and Mrs. Japon began making bread and the efficient way they went about it was a lesson to me.

A twenty-five-pound sack of flour, a frying pan or Dutch oven, a can of baking powder and a bucket of well water was the total of their equipment. They rolled back the top of the sack, put in a pinch of baking powder and mixed in enough water with their hands to make a dough stiff enough to handle easily. This was pulled and patted into a cake that covered the bottom of the cooking pan and fried in an inch or two of fat. The finished cakes were stacked in piles. It was an interesting performance; but after I had watched for a time, I realized they could not bake enough bread for the crowd that way, so I started to make biscuits in the oven. That was a full-time job. I learned then that one sack of flour just fills a washtub with biscuits.

While we women were preparing the bread, Ken had cut up the meat. Some women built up stones about the cooking fires to set tubs on, and soon we had three tubs of the meat simmering, each with an attendant stirring it with a long splinter of wood from the woodpile. The wash boiler did duty as a coffeepot. There was a forked cedar in it to hold the bag of coffee down. I was sure the whole dinner would be flavored with cedar, but it wasn't.

Other women I set to peeling onions and potatoes, and very handy they were at it too. These we added to the meat tubs. When everything was all well cooked, I mixed a pail of flour and water for thickening and added that, with salt, pepper and chili. The cooks tasted it often and said it was very good.

One of the children was sent out to the mesa edge to call the men; and in a few minutes they charged in, the ponies running pell-mell between the camp fires and jumping over the clutter of camp stuff, the Indians yelling like pirates and quirting on both sides. I never had heard a pirate yell, but I was sure a Navajo must be as good a yeller as a Comanche, and nothing else *could* make so much noise, unless it was a pirate.

The dripping ponies were left at one side and the Indians came to the fires. I dipped the stew into pans, all we had in the store; and then we passed tin cups of coffee and spoons for the stew. The family groups sat together and everybody ate and ate. Some of the heathen, I know, had not had a square meal for a month.

179

After the meal was over, the women cleaned the soot from the tubs and boiler with sand, while I scalded the spoons and pans. They were willing enough to do it, though they would have gone away and left everything dirty, if I had not suggested the dishwashing. I thought it best they do some little thing for their meal.

When that was done, the children lined up to get the bags of candy. I passed them out and soon became suspicious about the length of the line. Investigation revealed Mrs. Little Crank and a score of other mothers standing around the corner of the store, putting bags of candy into their blankets and sending the children back to stand in line for another. There was a sort of appreciation in the Navajo, but it was the sort that wanted all they could get from any one who wasn't looking.

By the middle of the afternoon they were all gone and we were allowed to eat something ourselves. Tired! But we agreed we had never seen such a Christmas and would not see another in a lifetime.

Among the last to go was Robert, who came to me and spoke in English, a thing he did not often do, as I had learned Navajo. "I wish you a Merry Christmas, San Chee (my name)," he said.

All day I had been too busy and excited to think, but that little attention made me homesick for something not Indian; and I stumbled into the store and hurried through to the living room, so Ken would not see the tears in my eyes.

He locked the store, polished the lamp chimney which I had not had time to touch and followed me. He set the lamp on the table and handed me an envelope.

"Merry Christmas," he said. He turned at once to undress and I knew he knew I did not want him to see me cry.

In the envelope was the receipt for the second payment on the farm.

"Ken," I gasped.

"Better get to bed. It's been a long day," he answered sleepily.

Half undressed, I sat on the edge of the bed. Outside a cold moon climbed to where I could see it through the window. We had been at Covered Water more than a year. Did Ken want to own a farm or would he rather stay on the reservation?

The moon climbed higher, and the shell of a house snapped and cracked in the cold. The air was freezing; I could see my breath in the moonlight, but still I sat.

I thought Ken asleep but suddenly he rolled over and spoke to me. When I faced him, he grinned at me in the moonlight.

With a gesture, I finished undressing and pulled the warm covers over me. My teeth were chattering and I blew out my breath sharply, to see the wraith of it in the moonlight. What difference whether we worked here or there, so we worked together?

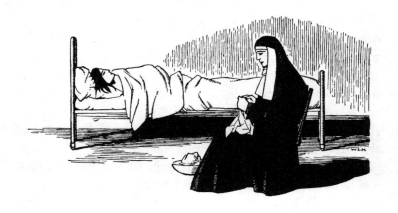

X · I GIVE UP

A WEEK after the Christmas celebration, a slow, heavy rain began, and in a day or two this was freezing. The wind blew so hard the snow and sleet seemed always on a horizontal level; one wondered how the flakes ever reached earth. I watched a few days and went to bed with such a pain as I did not know existed.

For days I believe I was scarcely conscious. Ken said later that I called almost continuously in a voice that grew weaker and weaker, "Ken — Ken — Ken." I seem to remember that, as if it were something someone else had done, and I remember that I could not eat.

Ken racked his brain to think of something new to bring me — all canned stuff, of course, as there was nothing else except meat. When I couldn't eat, he'd look so puzzled and woebegone and say, "But this, you've always liked this."

Tramp, tramp, tramp from the store to my bed and back again, he brought me everything from canned peaches to dill pickles. Frankfurters, tomatoes, canned beans, sauerkraut — they were all alike to me.

We had put a door in the doorway between the living room and the store and Ken kept this locked, so the heathen could not get to me, either to ask questions or to sympathize. Of course, every time he came to me during the day, he had to empty the store of loafers and customers and lock the outside door. Some Navajos take it for granted they are to help themselves to what is not at the moment being watched.

There was snow everywhere and the house was cold, in spite of the red-hot stove in the store and the cookstove in the living room. Icicles hung from the top of the window near my bed. I watched them lengthen, first this one the longest and then that one. I would bet with myself which would be ahead the next day and try to remember which had been longest the day before; but there were many days, and after I don't know how many dragging, uncounted ones had passed, the icicles seemed to grow together. I worried about it and made an effort to see them singly, and was relieved every time I realized I could still separate them. It seemed to be a job I was responsible for.

After ages, I seemed to be turning into an Indian; I was a deep, burnt orange color all over. My hair fell out and I ceased to care even about the icicles.

One night I knew the end was just beyond. I lay

thinking of Ken and the store and the work there was ahead and decided it would all have to go on without me. I was to die out there on the lonely reservation and be buried like a Navajo. It would be some rocky ledge and the stones would be piled high to protect me from the coyotes. The Indians always put dishes, baskets, and silver jewelry on a grave. What would be on mine? Nothing but rocks. How deep could a grave be dug in the frozen ground? That made me remember that some Indian had failed to bring back the shovel. How could Ken dig a grave without a shovel? It would be a hard job and I wouldn't be there to help; I'd better not make extra work.

If I died in this house, the store would be a total loss; no Navajo would ever step inside it again. The Indians might burn the house; that was their way. If I were inconsiderate enough to die, I would cause a deal of hard labor and a great financial loss. I decided against dying but somehow couldn't seem to take much action about the matter.

In the middle of that night a doctor arrived. He told Ken to get me a hot-water bottle. We did not have one. He said something about an operation, "If she lived to be moved to Gallup." Then he left some pink pills and went out.

I couldn't realize the doctor was important. What remained in my mind of his visit was Ken's face, as he stood in the lamplight beyond the doctor. It was unmoved, as always, but very white for so tanned a skin, and he was closely shaved. He was careful about shaving only when he particularly wanted to please me. I decided anew that I would stay with Ken, but that the doctor could help me never entered my mind.

The doctor stayed twenty minutes — price two hundred and twenty-five dollars. It was not too much for the trip. To put a big car over those terrible roads at that season was a feat in itself; but his advice was worthless and we had to borrow the money from the bank.

Ten days later, an Indian on horseback arrived with a hot-water bottle and we found that it was defective and leaked badly.

By the time the hot-water bottle arrived, I was better. It seemed to take forever to gain strength, but slowly I must have improved. The Indians, even the Old Buzzard, came to the window, broke off the icicles and shaded their eyes close up to the window to peer into the room and call to me. I tried to answer but couldn't get breath enough.

One day Ken left the living-room door unlocked and before I knew she was near, Mrs. Japon was sitting on the edge of my bed. All friendliness and crying softly while she talked, she took my hand and patted and rubbed it and my arm. I was weak as a sick cat, so I wept too, and wished Ken would come. I could not call loud enough to make him hear me, I knew; and, besides, it would not look well to call Ken to come to put my guest out. This little politeness held me until I saw a louse beside my arm on the bedspread. A long, gray Indian louse. On my bed! On me! There might be more. I was sure there were. And suddenly I found my breath and called. Ken came and got the visitor and louse and put them both outside. For days after that I felt things crawling on me but never found anything more.

It was springlike when I could walk. And how good the outdoors felt. Betty, who had spent most of the winter beside my bed, was almost frantic with joy.

As soon as I saw myself in the mirror, I cut off the few stringy wisps of hair I had left. Ken told me I looked like a Navajo sheared sheep. The weather was still decidedly chilly, so I made caps of the bright sateens in the store.

At last I was able to drag myself behind the counter and sit there, while Ken fed and watered the horses. The Indians seemed to know how weak I was and would not ask me to trade, but would wait patiently until Ken returned.

All of them were interested in my caps and my reason for wearing them. "My hair has run away," I told Hosteen En-Tso, "and my head is cold."

"All?" he asked.

"All," I answered, thinking to myself that I'd never go back to civilization bald; I'd stay on the reservation and wear sateen caps the rest of my life.

"It will come back," Hosteen En-Tso was assuring me. "To-morrow I will bring the medicine to help it grow and you make a cap for the woman at my home. Her head is cold too."

I promised the cap.

More days passed. Many of them. Thanks to Hosteen En-Tso's tonic, my hair was an inch long and curly. I could walk quite well and could wait on trade for a time each day — and then — if you've never had a toothache when you were a hundred miles from a dentist, you've missed something you should be thankful you've missed for the rest of your life. For a time I was aware of a nagging uneasiness in that tooth; then it began to demand more attention and at last it seemed I must go out to Gallup somehow. Ken had promised to look at another trading post whose owner wanted to sell. If he decided to buy it, we might leave Covered Water. He would want to spend some time watching the amount of trade at the new place. Whether he bought it or not, he had a month's riding to gather the cattle he had bought but that the wily Navajos had not delivered.

All this meant that I was needed badly at home; though with so little strength, I could not do my share and it was necessary to get some one to help in the store. This released me to make a trip to the dentist. By that time the roads were passable. Ken took me to Lugontale and there I took the mail stage to Gallup; because Lady Betty did not care for strangers and Ken could not console her, I took her with me.

I stayed with Ken's brother Fred and his family; it was so good to see them all again. However, I spent most of my time in the dentist's chair. He entertained me with tales of his experiences as sheriff twenty-five years before: how quick he could shoot and the intelligence of the horse he rode. He had an enlarged photograph of himself on his horse, hanging where his patients in the chair could not fail to see it. The horse was a proud iron-gray and the rider, hat, gun, spurs and all, seemed a part of him. I understood why he was proud of that picture. In it were the daring and courage and beauty of the West.

Half the men in town could remember when the railroad came through. I was really enjoying the change and the yarns when Ken's brother Jo and his wife from an even more distant trading post than Covered Water came to town for a few days' shopping. One afternoon I saw them off for the reservation with their big touring car loaded with boxes and packages and felt a pang of homesickness for Ken and the Indians.

I turned to climb the steep hill to Fred's house, that was temporarily home. Suddenly the old pain of the days when I watched the icicles hit me like a staggering blow. I stopped and looked up that steep street; there were gaps in the sidewalk before unimproved lots. At the end of each stretch of bare ground I would have to step up four to six inches to get on the sidewalk again. I made the first. On the next, I had to put my hands down on the sidewalk and was a long time getting my body upright again. The third step up I dared not risk. No one else was on the street. I walked out into the middle of the road and stayed there. Somehow I passed the vacant houses: somehow I got into our house and stood leaning against the door; then I fell on a bed and heard Mable at the 'phone, calling a doctor.

The doctor came; an operation, — but he did not want to do the work. He wired a surgeon in Albuquerque and got word back that he was caring for a maternity case and could not come for a day or two. Word was sent to Ken, — word that he would not receive for a week or more.

I GIVE UP

About three A.M., the local doctor came for me. The baby had arrived in Albuquerque and the surgeon was on his way to Gallup.

The hospital was only across the street. With the doctor's help, I walked that far and met the surgeon at the front door. I remember assuring him that I was not sick.

Catholic Sisters came to help me to bed and suddenly I realized that I was sick and very much needed help. I had never been near a Sister before and now I found myself crazily wondering if they understood English; the next moment I was thinking how unbearably hot and uncomfortable the white starched headdresses looked. Somehow I signed papers — I didn't know what — and gave the Sisters sixty dollars. That was not enough, but all I had with me, and since I was an emergency case, they agreed to take that on condition that I get in touch with my husband at once.

After that, there seemed to be nothing more I could do. I remember Fred and Mable had promised to send word to Ken.

I felt so useless and silly, riding on a wheeled stretcher to the surgery, with the Sisters walking beside; I said I could walk but they only smiled and said, "Every one rides."

I heard Dr. Kean's voice far away, telling me to breathe deep; then some one was calling me by name and saying that I was back in my own bed. It was the surgeon. I wanted to thank him for coming all the way from Albuquerque and wanted to ask how the new baby was, but I could not rouse myself.

One of the Sisters had a cot placed at right angles to my bed, the foot of the cot under the head of the bed.

At night she lay down fully dressed in the flowing habit and starched headdress. She snored loudly, the one sound I could not endure, and in her restlessness kicked the bed. When I asked her to take off the starched part of the headdress so that she could rest comfortably, she seemed quite shocked and said they did not remove any of their habit in public. I told her that the snoring and kicking were painful but she smiled and said I had not been conscious for four days and could not possibly have heard or felt anything. Nevertheless, she moved the cot that night.

To be comfortably sick was an experience I had not had before. The room was pleasant and heavenly clean; I was clean; and for the first time in years my hands were white and soft. The Sisters were most kind.

Tied to my bedside was a bottle with an attached rubber tube which extended to my gall bladder. I was told that it was sewed in with a stitch that would hold exactly eleven days. It did. In the tube was a glass section which, as the days passed, showed the changing color that flowed into the bottle. It was my daily entertainment to note the gradual improvement from the dark greenish color of old crank-case grease to amber, then clear as new honey, and on the eleventh day, as prophesied, the rubber tubing came out and I saw no more.

One day the doctor showed me a dark, rough, pear-shaped stone the size of an egg. He said that was the chief cause of the suffering; he was making a collection and asked if he might keep this extra fine specimen. He might.

When I could hold a book, I read; another and another and another and another.

I never saw women work harder or more uncomplainingly than the Sisters. If one sat beside me, she brought crochet hook and bureau scarf or towel. All the small linens had handwork on them, and now I understood how this had been done.

One morning the head Sister was almost jubilant. The street was being graded and the patron saint of the hospital had caused a wonderful stratum of sand to be found on the hospital property. This meant a great saving in putting in walks and drives. I rejoiced with the Sister, for I could see that the place was kept up chiefly by gifts and every saving meant much.

A few days later the street grade cut across the stratum of sand and the loose sand poured forth in an unceasing stream. A retaining wall would have to be built at great expense. The Sisters saw this as a punishment for their pride in possessing sand.

At another time a well-to-do patient who had entered the hospital, expecting never to leave it alive, left completely cured. He promised to send a gift. The Sisters who came to sit by me speculated on what the gift might be. Perhaps he would send chickens for their empty henhouse. Months earlier they had been short of meat for their patients and had killed the chickens. If only he would send a dozen hens. Perhaps he would furnish a vacant room.

And then the gift arrived. Thirty-seven goldfish in aquariums! There was grottoes, lighthouses, rocks, moss; there were fat fish and thin fish and flat fish; some had one tail fin and some seemed to have half a dozen. With them came a book, "Goldfish Culture." The Sisters silently handed me the book and I read and expounded. No one there had ever cared for goldfish and no one wanted to learn. They could have fried those goldfish with real enjoyment.

At last I could learn to walk again and needed a dressing gown. Two Sisters went shopping and brought back half a dozen gaily assorted ones. At a great gathering in my room a loud Japanese kimono, mostly blue, was selected. "I wish I dared slip it on, just for a moment," one pretty sister whispered to me. I made up my mind then and there she should do it some day when we were alone, but the opportunity never came.

I had written to Ken, but I knew his Indian fear of death. He had an almost equal fear of illness. The winter had been a nightmare to him. Now, since I had told him I was recovering, I waited for an answer while I learned to walk and while I put Irish picot edges on eight towels.

One month from the day I entered the hospital I walked out. I was a bit weak and shaky but quite free from pain.

Fred and Mabel welcomed me back into their home. How happy I was! If only Ken would write or come! I knew the others were wondering, and as the days became a week since I had left the hospital, I began to be embarrassed. In his life he expected action, accepted hardship; but he had only a blind fear of illness; still, why didn't he come?

Long after, I asked him if he would have come to my funeral if I had died. "No," he answered. "I would have ridden the other way." That hurt me but I knew it was true. Where he could really help, physically, he would not fail; where he could do nothing, he would ride hard to forget.

XI · HOME AGAIN

AGAIN Jo and his wife came to town. Again we shopped. Though the hill tired me, I stepped off and on the broken sidewalk and felt ever so proud of myself.

"We saw Ken at Chin Lee as we came in," they said. "Come back with us in the car and surprise him."

The doctor was dubious, but at last remarked that since I had made so much of a recovery in record time, I might risk it.

When I tried to express my gratitude to the dear people who had been family and friends during all the trying weeks, I felt helplessly dumb — but I think perhaps they understood what I could not say.

Into the rear seat of the big touring car I was wedged, with Betty and a case of eggs to keep us all from bouncing. Bundles were piled in every possible cranny.

HOME AGAIN

That drive! I was well and we were outward bound. The reservation again. I had not realized I loved it so. We sang. I had not heard another voice join with mine for ages, not since Oregon and the days in the choir of the church there. We sang all the old hymns we knew and there were dozens. I was happier than I could remember having been ever before. I was taking health and strength back to Ken. I would not be the burden I had been all winter.

At noon there was lunch under a piñon tree and a nap for me. For supper there was a camp fire, coffee, toast, opened cans of things. We ate with the wall of dark close around us.

We were not following the road to Black Mountain but were going to Chin Lee, where the others had seen Ken as they had come in from their own trading post, miles farther west. Here was a mountain range to descend. We waited for the white moonlight, before making the descent, and then started down from rocky shelf to rocky shelf, I holding Lady Betty clasped tightly to me to prevent what jarring I could. Common sense whispered to take care of myself, though I felt nothing in the world would get me down again. I wanted never to take off my clothes or go to bed.

The mountain was a study in black and white, the white moonlight on the light rock surfaces making the shadows inky black. One moment our lights glowed against huge tumbled masses of rocks or piñon trees as still as the night itself and almost as dark as the darkness, and the next the lights were a thin pale beam that faded away into the nothingness that was space. I tilted my head back to look at the stars. They were yellow and far away and quiet in an Arizona-blue night sky and I felt that everything in the world was absolutely right.

At midnight we reached Chin Lee, where our shouts brought the trader to the door. We told him who I was and he called Ken. Before the others, Ken and I clasped hands as two Indians might have done. When we were alone, he said, as I stretched out wearily beside him, "I'm getting up at four o'clock to get an early start. You won't need to stir."

After a week at Chin Lee, while Ken finished his riding, he and I returned to Black Mountain. Here we found Lem Dimelson still in charge, and here I learned that all my sickness and suffering had been caused by that bear's visit; the Indians knew all the time that some disaster must follow that.

Old Blue Goat, a good friend and most solicitous, told me how sad they were when Ken told them that the doctor had opened my body with a knife. And was it really a stone the doctor took out? A stone? How had I happened to swallow a stone? I hadn't enough Navajo to tell the old fellow how a gallstone happened, even if I had known, so I could only repeat over and over that I did not swallow it. He looked puzzled, patted me and held my hand.

The Old Lady and her daughters came to welcome me home and announce that Robert had returned for good from his visit with his own people and had married his dead wife's younger sister and was again established as the Old Lady's son-in-law.

Nothing surprised me more than the gift of a young

kid from the Old Buzzard herself. I was truly touched when she brought the little creature in under her arm and said it was for me to make a pet of, because it would make me laugh again. We named him at once Billy the Kid, and he began his entertainment by playing about the house and jumping and scampering through the place after Betty, who did not know whether to be indignant or to join in the chase. Billy took his morning exercise the moment he could dash in from the tent where we made him stay at night. A flying leap landed him on the table; from there across the sewing machine and to my dresser, where he would slip and knock over every bottle. The next jump took him to the narrow window sill, where he leaned like a race horse rounding a curve, until he bounded into the middle of the bed; this he kicked into a heap as he spurned the covers and jumped over the foot rod onto the trunk and from there to the stove; whether this was hot or cold, he only stayed a fraction of a second before a leap landed him on my work shelf and another across the doorway to the table again; and on around the circuit, with Betty barking in the middle of the room because she couldn't follow him.

It was several days before I discovered that Billy the Kid had lice. I rubbed him with a cloth wet in kerosene but was afraid of using too much and taking the hair off.

"I'd rather be bald than have lice," I insisted.

"But maybe Billy wouldn't," laughed Ken, and since that did seem to be Billy's sentiment, we turned him over to the Old Lady's flock where *yaas* were in style.

First Aid

I gained strength rapidly and leaped eagerly to meet the old life. I had not dreamed I would miss it so. We were in the midst of another wool season and I felt at home and needed and was happy.

On my first full day behind the counter I made the alarming discovery that we were almost out of baking powder. How could any one run a store without baking powder? A fifteen-cent can went with every twenty-five-pound sack of flour. I could hear myself saying despairingly, "*Aigizy beth-thay-lin atin.*" (Really there is no baking powder). I underlined an extra case on our list for supplies that the next freight teams would take out to Gallup. Wool was coming in fast; there would soon be a trip out for somebody.

One day the Little Bidoni came to us with two such loads of wool as he had hauled to Chin Lee the year before. Within a week he was back with the second two loads; and as his horses and mule teams were strong and his wagons in good repair, Ken again persuaded him to take our loads and drive in to Gallup for a return load of supplies.

The fifteen-year-old son of the Little Bidoni's oldest wife sat perched high on a load of woolsacks and drove four mules, his own team, the Little Bidoni told Ken.

The boy flashed a friendly grin to every one and was popular with others beside his own family. We called him Nazhuni Yazzi, Little Handsome. Ken had fixed a gun for him, even before we knew whose hogan he came from, and so we had earned his everlasting admiration. He always wore the brightest red silk bandeau with a rosette knot and dainty fringe that swung like a little tassel in front of his left ear; his teeth were perfect and white; his eyes coal black and soft; his velvet tunic and silver belt, his beads and moccasins, all made such a perfect picture of the Navajo at his highest and best that just seeing and knowing the child raised the whole tribe in our respect and regard.

By the time the wool was unloaded, a top buggy had arrived with the boy's mother and her distinguished father and head of the family, Hosteen Utcity himself, in all his velvet and turquoise. They camped for the night in our hogan a few steps from the store, and because I wanted an excuse to see the woman's camping equipment, I offered her a loaf of bread. I found her sitting on the ground beside a tiny fire in the middle of the hogan. She was cutting steaks from a whole carcass to broil on a wire grid that she had set over the piñon fire. When I gave her the bread; she thanked me and cut off two more steaks and gave them to me, saying, "For your man and you. I killed this fat goat this morning." I took the meat gratefully; these were real folks.

In the early morning there was hustle and running about to get the outgoing wagons loaded. Dried hides of sheep, goats, cattle and horses had to be sorted and piled flat and tied into bales with two or three tugging Indians standing on them to compress the straggling rawhide ends and pull the tie ropes snug.

The most precious part of the freight was, of course, the Navajo blankets, each with its special tag and record of weaver and purchase. These were baled in burlap and securely sewed so that not a yarn of them was visible, and then the bales were placed in the middle of the load of hides, so that there was many a water-tight covering in case of rain and nothing outwardly visible to tempt some bankrupt gambler into one more game, if he had a salable blanket.

Nazhuni Yazzi came driving in the mules and horses which had been hobbled for the night out on the mesa; the drove went clattering down the hill past the store, and Indians ran to make guard lines to head them into the corral. With whooping and dust, the gate was shut on the drove and Nazhuni Yazzi rode his sweating pony up to the store door for further instructions. I was standing on the loading platform beside Utcity, while Ken and two Navajos tied down the load of hides with heavy ropes that went through iron loops on the wagon box.

"Next, what, Grandfather?" the boy smiled. "Is it time to put the harness on these with the long ears?"

Grandfather beamed, "Yes, the mules' load is ready now. See the white man has put his highest-priced load on your wagon, my grandson. Under these hides there are hidden two large sewed-close bundles of blankets. Bring up the mules quickly; we will put on the harness at once." He waved the boy away. I could not take my eyes from the child. There just never was such a perfect figure.

I said to Utcity, "My grandfather, I have a name for your grandson; do you want to hear it?"

The rugged old man looked down at me and smiled.

"Yes," he said, "what is it? His mother and his grandmother have so many names for him that one more won't matter to the gods."

I knew how they must feel in the home hogans and laughed.

"My husband and I call him Nazhuni Yazzi, the child who is beautiful inside and outside."

Utcity nodded. "He is what you say — we try not to spoil him — "

"Aye-ie-" a shout of terror and disaster sounded from the corral. We looked quickly in that direction to see the drove of animals huddled in one corner where a man stood, looped lariat swung limp from a motionless arm. On the ground lay Nazhuni Yazzi, his lariat snarled beside him.

Ken cleared the load of pelts with one leap and started running. No one else had moved. I started but Utcity took hold of my arm and turned me to the door. "Into the house and stay," he said sternly. From my window I saw Ken reach the corral fence, when the Little Bidoni seized his arm and stopped him. They came back to the store with the Navajos who were standing about the yard. Some one went to the camp hogan and at once the Little Bidoni's wife came toward the store, her shawl pulled high about her head. She did not once look toward the corral. I could see the huddled heap that was Little Handsome and I couldn't be sure that all the scarlet I saw was the red bandeau. I was frantic. Utcity was undoubtedly boss of the situation and he called on a specialist. Untiligi was there, and he had been merely an onlooker; but now at a word from Utcity,

Untiligi, who was not related to the boy at all, went out alone.

With a little medicine bag in his hand he walked slowly to the corral gate. There he stood for an hour, or five minutes — one can't estimate time under such circumstances — and then he zigzagged into the corral, sprinkling medicine out of the bag. When he reached the boy, he took pinches of something out of the bag and dropped them on or around Little Handsome. He made motions in the air, as if he were driving something away.

It was about ten minutes before he stooped down and helped the boy to his feet. The lad walked slowly and painfully about. The doctor followed him, making signs and pushing something imaginary away. They came out of the corral, went by the house and disappeared over the hill.

The family went outside but made no move to go near the boy. After a little the mother followed the child but came back almost at once. Ken walked around where he could see and found the boy lying on the ground, out of sight of the camp hogan. We waited and watched and surely the Indians must have been doing the same; but there was not the least appearance of uneasiness or watchfulness on the surface. The father was not in sight; the mother sat quietly on our floor, with her shawl over her head.

It was an hour before the men all went out to the corral to rope and harness the horses and mules.

The light and fun were gone from the morning's work for every one.

HOME AGAIN

Just when I thought I could not stand it another moment, the Little Bidoni's wife stood up; I went to her and asked if I could go to the boy with her, and she took my hand and we went out together over the hill.

Nazhuni Yazzi lay on the ground in front of the camp hogan door. Hosteen Untiligi, standing near and facing east, was chanting in a low, husky voice.

The boy smiled up at his mother and said, "I am well, my mother. Tell my father I will drive the team to-day." Little Bidoni's wife squeezed my hand. "It is not time to start yet, my son; rest until you are called. It is well; all is well," and she went quietly about, packing up the camp pots and rolling the bed pelts for loading.

I looked at Untiligi; he did not see me when I leaned over the boy and whispered, "Does it hurt anywhere?"

Nazhuni Yazzi smiled up a brave, kiddish grin and said, "That mule is a devil in the hind legs. I guess my head is very hard. Will you tell the men that I will drive my team? Will you?"

"Yes," I said, "I'll tell them right away," and I went back to the house.

It was not until Untiligi came in and said that the boy could go but must ride in the buggy until the noon stop, that we really felt comfortable again.

The teams got away at last, the Little Bidoni ahead, Utcity driving the mules, and Nazhuni Yazzi and his mother in the top buggy, bringing up the rear. Not one look of disappointment in the boy's face. No Indian had questioned or argued with the doctor on the case, but I said to Ken, "I wonder if the boy should have gone?" Ken shrugged his shoulders and turned to put out a can of tomatoes and a box of crackers for Untiligi. The rest stood back respectfully and he ate them all. The day's work went on.

A Sand Painting

It was in July that I saw another healing ceremony as remarkable as Hosteen Untiligi's treatment of Little Handsome.

One Sunday morning I saw Ken off after cattle immediately after breakfast. I brushed around as little as my conscience would permit, washed my hair and sat down to write letters.

At that moment the Old Lady and her two daughters came to call and borrow beads, bracelets and a medicine basket for a big "sing." The Old Lady herself was to be the patient. All through the spring and early summer she had complained of pains in her back and shoulders. She had been doing an unusual amount of weaving, all of it remarkably beautiful even for her, whose work was the best in the Black Mountain country, but she did not think the long hours at the loom cause enough for her pain; there must be a *chindi* (devil) responsible for part of it.

The next morning I went to the ceremony, which began with a sand painting. I was determined to get a picture of that if it could be done, but alas for my efforts. The painting covered the whole floor of the hogan and the only light in the room was the bright spot of sun through the smoke hole. I could not get far enough away to get a lateral view, so climbed up the outside of the hogan and snapped through the smoke hole.

HOME AGAIN

The picture was poor, but I felt that the two dollars I paid for the privilege of taking it was a low price for what I saw.

I went early and found the high and mighty medicine man. Untiligi, arranging a cushion of green boughs and ripe grass. When he had finished that, he made a big suds of yucca root in a basket. This he placed before the boughs and sprinkled both with powdered leaves of some sort. All the time he was singing, and other singers with rattles sang with him.

Now the Old Lady took off her shirt and moccasins and knelt on the green boughs. The medicine man took down her hair, took off her beads, wet her head, and then washed her beads while she washed her hair. He poured the rinse water over her head. Never before had I seen an Indian man make himself useful to a woman in the least degree.

When her head was washed, he washed her feet and sprinkled her back; and I began to think he was going to help her off with the only skirt she had on; but three women came in and held robes to make a screen while the Old Lady finished her bath to the music the singers kept up.

After the bath, they told me there would be nothing more to see for a time, and I could go home and come back again about noon. I did. It was when I returned at noon that I saw the sand painting. It was so large there was barely space to sit one-deep around the walls of the hogan.

It was done in black, white, red, blue and yellow sand, and was beautiful beyond anything I had expected. The design was four stalks of corn, representing the corn god, with ears and silk on each. On top of each stalk was a square head with arms and hands, one hand holding a large ear of corn and the other a ball. On each top corner of the head there was a tassel and on top of each tassel was a bird, and a good bird he was too. Around the foot and the two sides of the whole was a framelike stripe with corner posts of turkey and eagle feathers. Every line of the entire picture was clear and perfect.

At one side the Old Lady sat on a pile of new calico covered with buckskin. She was without shirt and shoes. While the chorus kept up a steady song, the doctor painted her. A dazzling sight she was.

The colors were mixed very thin and smooth by rubbing little balls of colored clay on smooth, flat stones, dipping the clay balls in water and rubbing again. When all was mixed, the doctor touched the white paint with his forefingers and, singing high and shrill all the while, in time with his painting, he made a double row of polka dots down each of the Old Lady's arms, then hit and miss over her back and down the front. He duplicated the performance with blue paint and then with yellow, until there was only a pleasing background of brown skin showing.

Still using the two paint fingers, he drew a black line straight across her face through the eyebrows. Her face above this he made a dead white. From the black line down to and including her upper lip, he made a solid yellow; her face below this and about half her neck he painted black. No one could possibly have recognized my dear and respected neighbor. Her beautiful black hair was wet and dangling and had bits of herb sprinkled through it.

All this was hard work for the doctor. He weighed two hundred and twenty-five and was stooping and singing constantly. The perspiration dripped from his face, and his plush shirt showed dark, wet areas where the moisture came through.

It seemed to me there was not much more he could do in the way of decorating the Old Lady, but he knew something else. He moved his paint stone down to her feet and, still chanting gustily, he squatted on his heels and, dipping small feather brushes in the paints, he made a snake on each foot. The heads in white with black mouth, nose and eyes were on each great toenail; the white zigzag angles of the bodies ran halfway up the shin bone. Her skirt was folded back barely far enough to allow for the painting.

When all was finished, no one could have called her naked; she was actually the most covered-up person I ever looked at. Comical! I wanted both to laugh and to weep. My poor dignified Old Lady — and every one so sober.

While all this was being done, an assistant had been covering a ten-year-old boy with black and white polka dots. It seemed he was being taught the ceremony.

The decorated ones were now seated in the middle of the picture where the doctor waved feathers, shells, sticks of all sorts over them, and finally tied a bunch of feathers like a toy duster to the Old Lady's topknot. She looked as rakish as anything with all that paint she was wearing. Then he took two little boards with gods painted on them, and, clapping her between them, he twisted her body to the right and then to the left, all the time making a sort of thrilling noise that almost wrecked my gravity. He did that with every doo-dad he had in his pack, and then went over the lot again.

She sat with her legs straight out in front of her, and he placed boards at the soles of her feet and then gave each foot a little kick; with a trill he brought feather dusters down on her head; finally he put around her neck a necklace of dried and braided corn husk and put bracelets of the same on her arms. After he had done everything any one could possibly think of, he sent the two painted ones out. Then he put the handle of the feather-duster affair in his mouth, took a bunch of eagle feathers in one hand and blew the whistle in the handle of the duster, as he dragged the feathers down a line of the painting. In this way he went down each corn stalk and around the border.

This being finished, a robe was spread down in the middle of the floor and the two patients — victims would be a better word — were called back. A basket of corn meal, with a pattern in medicine powder drawn on top, was set before them. The doctor took a pinch about as big as an egg and shoved it into the Old Lady's mouth. Somehow she managed to get it down in time for the next. After that, she and the boy helped themselves for a little — and that act was over.

They asked me to have some of the corn meal and I tasted it. No salt! How they ever swallowed it, I didn't see!

I found two *yaas* when I took a bath immediately

after reaching home. And those two little *yaas* were very hungry. By the way, *yaa* is Navajo for louse.

I did not dare ask any questions during the ceremony and I was truly impressed with the earnestness and the complicated ritual of the whole affair. Afterwards I inquired and found out that the colored sands were rocks and earths from the Painted Desert, ground fine by hand on the stone mills, such as the Hopi uses for his corn-grinding.

The dry, fine sand was held between thumb and finger close over the smooth background of the red desert sand; and the fine delicate lines and patterns could only be carried out in a perfectly draftless and protected, thick-walled hogan.

As a part of the ceremony, these sand pictures were always destroyed before sundown; therefore, one never saw them except in all their perfection.

I watched anxiously for signs of physical improvement in the Old Lady and tried to believe with her that when the paint spots wore off her body, she would be rested and strong again. For several weeks she did no weaving but gave more attention to the children; and because I had an extra barrel and allowed Robert to fill and haul it to her hogan, she did not carry so much water by head strap and sling as she was accustomed to do.

All the Navajos believed that the medicine of our friend Hosteen Untiligi was potent and that the Old Lady was permanently improved.

XII · IMMEDIATE ATTENTION

OF course, Ken and I thought the rest was helping the Old Lady and wished that our friends had spent their energy and skill on prayers for rain. Many ponds were dry. Stock were dying of thirst. The sand was deep and deeper and the freight teams slow and slower.

I wished one had never arrived. It brought word from the bank that our note was overdue. "Please give this your immediate attention." We were borrowing money at twelve per cent. to pay on the farm.

Ken was away helping the Indian men to extend dams and showing them where to build new ones, so that more water could be stored when the rains came. "Immediate attention!"

My immediate attention was attracted to an uproar

outside. I reached the window in time to see an old hen defending her chicks against a Navajo dog. I yelled at the dog; the hen squawked. Before I could get close, he had bitten the rear half of her body off. She struggled a few steps, clucking feebly to her chicks — and died. The dog ran down to the well, where Cla and some men he had brought from Saluni were scraping the well dry with a tin can to water their horses.

The well was at the foot of the hill and the dog ran among the men. Not a good shot, but I was too furious to hesitate. I ran for the gun. My first shot dropped the dog and scattered the Indians. I followed with two more shots, to make sure the dog was dead. In a second or two not a Navajo was in sight. When fifteen or twenty minutes had passed and I had done no more shooting, Robert entered the store.

I gave him the gun and sent him to see if the dog was dead. He did not have to shoot.

"They are gone and will never come again," he reported concerning Cla and his crowd. I didn't care. Cla was a good riddance any time, and the departure of his friends gave me no tendency to relieve the general drouth with tears.

For a couple of days the Navajos were good-mannered beyond belief. They whispered their requests for a quarter's worth of sugar and whispered to each other that I was *"hoski do hy yea"* (very angry). No one mentioned the dog except Ken, when he returned. He thought my killing worse news than the note from the bank. "It might lead to the burning of the store and the end of us," he told me.

The please-kind-friend manners were not interrupted by an attack on us, but by a domestic upheaval in the Japon family. We thought we had seen Mrs. Japon at her most vigorous and best, only to learn that she could exceed all her past efforts.

Hosteen Japon, with his first lady's hearty approval apparently, spent most of his time at a hogan near Saluni, with a younger and prettier, if less capable wife.

Our Mrs. Japon and her sixteen-year-old daughter, Bedazi, were on the way to the store in a wagon. The second Mrs. Japon, who had no children and was jealous of the older wife, rode up horseback beside the wagon and lashed the girl three or four times across the back and shoulders with a rope's end.

Probably the things the older woman said brought the younger one to a realization of the position in which she had placed herself, for she arrived at the store with her horse covered with lather. She was panting and wanted to buy a gun. When we would not sell her one, she ran crazily around the living room, hunting a place to hide. As she realized there was no place of concealment there, she heard the rattle and bang of a wagon and looked out the window to see the older Mrs. Japon standing up in her wagon, lashing her horses into a dead run. The wagon was hitting all the rocks while Bedazi sat flat on the wagon bed and held on to the side.

The younger woman ran out the rear door, through the wool tent and disappeared, running like a rabbit through the piñons toward the Old Lady's hogan.

Our Mrs. Japon stormed into the store and had seen every person in there before we could turn around twice. She was swinging a quirt and was the most furious person I ever saw. What a lecture every man in that store did get and how quietly they stood and took it. I couldn't understand all she said, but how I wished I could. She was built like an Irish washerwoman and had a baby a month old — her eighth.

The men in the store included Ken, Untiligi, her husband, her brother and a number of others. She was no respecter of persons. I understood enough of what she said to gather what she thought of a person who would strike a child, and of men who let such a person live, etc., etc. She said she didn't have babies to pound up; she nursed and loved them, and not one of them had ever been struck until this —— ! —— ! —— ! woman had hit her little girl; she was going to kill her with her own hands. She went on to tell the men more of their shortcomings and general inadequacy. I got about a third of it, but she could have been no more eloquent in any language; of that I am sure.

Not a man, not even her husband, so much as lifted an eyelash. You'd have thought the husband did not know anything was happening. Perhaps that was his best or only protection.

At last she quieted a little and began to trade but punctuated the job with venomous outbursts that kept the men busy trying to look unconscious. After she had gone, Japon sneaked out and we did not see him or the second wife for months. I was glad it was not Mrs. Japon's dog I had killed.

Self-Defense

The fall of 1916 Ken rode often and late for cattle. One morning he was gone by daylight, gray daylight, which was too early for me. I slept another two hours before I was disturbed by some one shaking the door. If the store door was locked, the heathen seemed to be irritated, and pounded and hammered until they got in; but they would then have all the time in the world and couldn't be driven away.

Some such busy person was my alarm clock. He and his like spent the day looking at the store, and I spent most of it looking at them.

While I was eating my supper with one eye still on the store, a rib of roasted kid in one hand and a book in the other, the trusty Old Man came into the front door and straight through into my room, where he knew I didn't like to have any one come, unless the occasion was momentous or confidential. I gave him a rib, a slice of bread and a cup of tea. He was very sober and settled down to the meal as if he were doing me an honor.

He spoke seriously, almost solemnly, while he nibbled the bread and sipped the tea loudly. "There is much trouble coming, my daughter. It is not good, not good at all that you are a woman and here alone."

Thinking that this was to be a lecture on the reasons why I should not be left alone in charge of the post without paying him to guard both me and the valuables, I waited.

"The *deneh* (Navajos) are all my friends," I remarked. "The men surely know I am not afraid. They call me their friend and sister. Why should I fear my brothers? I make their shirts; I make coats and vests for them; I give them food. Which one among them would harm me, my father?"

The Old Man was really worried, and what I said did not cheer him up. "My daughter speaks the truth," he said slowly, "but what man will remember these things after he is full of strong *toh-dis-clish* (whisky)? Listen. They gamble at Untiligi's hogan. They have been at the cards until many have no money or silver left to play. All have had much whisky."

"Who gave them the whisky?" I broke in. "Where did they get it?"

"Nobody knows, my daughter; but they are drunk now and do not know friend or enemy. All they know or want now is to come here and take away their pawned silver, so they may gamble again. The talk is that they will come to-night."

I felt a bit weak and thought of Ken riding after cattle almost anywhere within a forty-mile circle and no way of reaching him. I tried to seem indifferent.

"Do the *deneh* know that Ken is away?"

"Yes, they know. He was seen far away this morning and he was driving cattle."

"They are not drunk enough to come to rob if he were here, are they?" I asked, trying to find out just how serious the situation was and thinking to myself that the old man had a good deal of silver with us himself, and I had known him to gamble too.

The Old Man sipped loudly and held the rib bone

daintily, turning it round and round, to study it from all sides. "The *deneh* are drunk. They want their beads and turquoise, their silver bracelets and other things that are here. They are gambling and must have them. You have always been good to them; you have given them food and made their shirts on your fast sewing machine. Perhaps they think that if they all come together, you will give them the silver; but they will wait until they are so drunk they will not care if you refuse. Some of them will hold you quietly, and the others will take what they need from the pawn box. La-a-a, my daughter, talk does not stop *deneh* when they have whisky."

I admit I didn't feel any too sure that he was not right about it, but no use weakening. I poured out some tea and laughed a little.

"Thanks, my father, for telling me these things. You have been a true friend to me. Certainly these drunken *deneh* shall not know that you have warned me. I will not at any time tell them of to-day."

The Old Man finished his tea, wiped his mouth with the back of his hand and said, "It is good. I will lie at the woodpile to-night. I will come after all is quiet. It will not be safe for me to go to the camp hogan, for the robbers may go there. It is best that I take a rifle with me and conceal it in the chips, in case of need." He reached for the gun rack, but that was too much for me.

I said, "No guns, no shooting. These *deneh* are all my friends. If they are so drunk they have to be shot, I will do it, my father. You must not shoot your own kind."

He gave me a queer look and said, "Your man would

want me to have the rifle. Things may be very bad."

The more eager he was to have the gun, the more uncertain I was which side he would use it on. "Things would be very bad for me," I said, "if I let any one have the big rifle. My man would be angry because he lets only me keep it cleaned and loaded."

"Oh, do you keep it cleaned and loaded?"

"Yes, always," I answered. "It is loaded and clean at all times. We keep all the guns loaded and clean, but they will not be needed to-night. When the drunken ones come, I will talk to them. If I have trouble making them understand, do you come and bring your son-in-law, Robert, for interpreter — "

"*A-la-honi,* my daughter, my son-in-law, Robert, is in the gambling crowd and is very drunk." He shook his head doubtfully and went away, muttering.

I spent the next hour moving all the calico-wrapped rolls of pawn into Betty's box. There wasn't room left for her, unless she lay on top of them, so I put her sheepskin on top. She tried her bed and didn't like it, but grunted resignedly. She used the two canvas money bags for a pillow but did not appreciate a bumpy mattress of bridles and belts.

Dark came. I went outside to reconnoiter about the post. Everything was absolutely still and so black I couldn't see even a sky line. I walked slowly, stopping every few steps to listen. The corrals were empty and still, but for the chickens talking to each other. I turned the flash light into their dugout. Ken had both horses with him. I was glad of that, because one alone would fret himself into a frenzy.

I climbed painfully through the rough picket fence surrounding our little haystack and walked slowly around it. No one. I went around the big ware tents to the camp hogan and flashed the light in there. Empty. I walked around the two pelt tents, where there were several hundred pounds of dried hides, easy to steal. I went into the flour tent and marked with a crayon all the upper and outer sacks so we could identify the empty sacks, in case we ever saw them full again. After that, stopping often to listen, I went to the wells and with a box board smoothed out the sand around each, so a new track would be plain. Then I came back into the room and lighted the lamp.

I certainly would not sit in the dark, though the Old Man thought I should. I wondered just what story, if any, he took back to the gambling party. Did I bluff them or didn't I?

The store part of the building was dark. One rifle lay on the end of the counter near some cases of canned goods. These I stacked up a little higher than my head. I hoped no one would make the tomatoes leak; we had only one case left. The other rifle I put at the other end of the store, across the hundred-pound sack of pea-nuts. By climbing up on two hundred pounds of sugar, I could see out the high window and watch the hay-stack, which was good cover for any one on that side.

The shotgun and the revolver I placed on the table beside me. All the ammunition we had for each gun was in a box beside it. There was nothing I could do to keep bullets from coming through the thin shell of a house. I kept telling myself not to be scared before I was hurt

— but how quickly that place would burn down. It could be set with one match. One layer of boards and a tar-paper roof, and all perfectly dry. There wouldn't be a pailful of ashes, if the whole thing burned.

Betty wanted to go to bed. She tried to climb into my lap, but when she saw the guns on the table, her ears dropped down; she gave me a scared and reproachful look and tried to scratch down the covers of my bed and get into that. I was scared too. The guns on the table scared me more than ever.

I took one more walk around outside with the flash light and called it a day. It was after midnight. "If I should die before I wake — " I lay down to take a nap with both ears and an eye open.

When I woke, the sun was shining. As I dressed, I looked into the store, trying to calculate how long it would take me to take down my fort of canned goods. The first thing I saw made me forget the canned goods. The front door was wide open. For two seconds I was paralyzed. I thought they had come and I had not wakened. Impossible! A glance revealed that nothing had been touched. I sat down by the table and laughed the most soul-easing laugh I ever had — and needed.

When I had gone out on that last round of inspection, I had come in by the tent and had forgotten all about the front door, which I had left open as I went out!

And the work I did that day! I got to moving the tomatoes about and decided I might as well sweep up a bit. Then I stacked up the flour, twenty-five-pound sacks only, into a neat new pile and changed the shoes from one shelf to another. I cleaned out all the odds and ends of pawn rolls under the counter and piled them back in half the space. I opened new boxes and filled all the shelves; I washed the glass of our only show case and put a lot of Tiffany turquoise and new silk scarfs on display.

I washed my hair and made lemon pies and cookies. A few Indians came in, and I shook hands with them all and passed out canned peaches and a box of crackers — and smokes, of course. It was a large day. All the time I worked, I could see the joke on myself and I could scarcely wait until Ken got back to see all I'd done.

I waved gaily at the Old Man when he appeared. I hoped he slept as well as I had — and I was glad I saw that open front door before he did.

And the end of the day! How different from the day before! I went out to look at a sky all shades of flame and pink. I had not known we had a sunset the night before, even though it probably covered the circle of the sky with a glory of color.

At last I heard Teddy calling. He was loose and coming home ahead. Ken and Witte were close behind. I knew the ponies would be glad to get home, and I had my pockets full of cookies for them and my head full of a story for Ken.

He asked questions, looked wise and listened. Then he just stood very quiet, with his hand on my shoulder. After I had finished, we had supper; and a darkness that was quiet and safe and lovely came down about us.

I had not remembered that overdue note at the bank for twenty-four hours, and we did not speak of it that evening; but the next morning I asked Ken what we could do. Something had to be found.

"Taylor's coming out any day now, you know, to select the site for the new store building. Perhaps we can get a loan from him."

Mr. Taylor did come and with him was a Mr. Bruce, a Baltimore man and a fancier of Navajo blankets.

"I told Bruce the best weaver on the reservation is a neighbor of yours and you are the sort of traders who would have some of her blankets put away," and Taylor introduced his guest.

"We have five of the Old Lady's on hand now," I said. "They are too rare to go out on the freight loads."

"Fine, fine," Mr. Taylor beamed. "Good work; that's the way to watch your business. Now while you show Bruce the five best blankets on the reservation, I will just look around with Ken here, and we'll pick out the site for the new store building. How's that after a year and a half in this place, eh?"

It was wonderful to think we should have a real building at last. I laughed and waved Mr. Taylor and Ken out of doors. "Don't go far," I begged. "I've grown to like this location very much."

Mr. Bruce was fascinated with the marvelous blankets. How lovely they looked spread out over the wide counter in the mellow light from the high windows. The colors and figures were typical, perfectly Indian, and the work of an artist. The diamond patterns were like mosaic, melting into the backgrounds of other diamonds. There was an individuality that made them easily the work of the same person, and yet two of the blankets had been made by Slender Girl and Robert's wife. In fact, I told Mr. Bruce that I had watched all three women work at the same time on the largest blanket. They sat side by side before the loom, while each worked on a different elevation of the weaving, but every corner of every diamond finished in the exact spot intended and completed a perfect design.

He asked if the blankets were all for sale, and remembering the bank note that was due, I replied that they were. I had clung to one of the small blankets for months, in the hope that I could have it for my own. At once it was settled in Mr. Bruce's mind that the blankets were his. He would speak to Mr. Taylor and take them with him.

When Mr. Taylor and Ken returned and announced that, after walking all about within a reasonable radius of the well, they had decided to put the new building directly in front of the old one, I was delighted.

The blanket arrangement was completed, and I hastened to write a letter to the bank in which I enclosed a check that relieved our anxiety about the note and made the farm ownership closer.

It was late when we said good-by to Mr. Taylor and his friend and, regretfully on my part, to the Old Lady's blankets.

XIII · HOPI

THE fall of 1916 was the hottest autumn weather we experienced on the reservation. With a dry wind blowing much of the time, we felt sand every time we moved. It was on our tongues, in the dishes, in my hair. In a few minutes there was so much grit on the fresh sheets of sticky fly paper I put out that the flies used them for a trotting park.

We had six weeks of that burning weather, and six weeks of Arizona sunshine at that season destroyed so much late pasture that we despaired of having hay enough to last the horses through the winter. The grass was burned and all the water holes were baked. Our well was kept dipped dry, scraped with a cup. Stock wandered everywhere and died anywhere. All night horses pawed our well curb; cattle wandered up the wash, bawling; sheep bleated and moaned in the corrals.

At last one day we saw clouds in the offing and could tell by the air that it was raining — somewhere in Arizona. The Indians reported day by day that water holes were filling up, but stock crowded to them and drank them dry again and again.

Suddenly it began raining at the post and in five minutes we were as busy as muskrats. The store roof leaked in six places. In no time I had tubs of rain water — and then I had more than tubs full, that I did not need. My back entry was a tent. There I kept the oil barrel and the washbench; there Ken kept the wool frames with sacks attached; there we kept everything we could not find another place for. When the rain started, my sewing machine was in the midst of the tent and its clutter, where I had dragged it to find the coolest place. The water ran down the hill and into the tent in a stream. Everything that could float, did. A government veterinarian was with us at the time and he and I dashed madly about, anchoring things, setting out pans and tubs, and grabbing shovels to try to turn the water.

Ken ran to the tent where the flour and grain were stacked and we heard a call for help. The doctor ran with his shovel and I stayed and mopped and poured and drained. A stream was running into the corral. The thunder was so close that the Indians in the store were frightened and did not approve when I laughed and said it was pretty. They did not think it was either pretty or funny for *"Ah-ditni"* (thunder) to come in the house. Just the same, some of the rascals stole a shovel or two and went running to the flats to drown out prairie dogs.

It was all over in an hour. The men came back from the cellar, where they had moved about a carload of flour and grain out of the drip. It had been a real cloud-burst. Our wash was boiling full and I walked down to where it emptied into the big wash farther out in the valley to see the sights and was surprised beyond words at the amount of water. The flood was washing out dams and cornfields and the Japon hogans. The big arroyo, that was twenty feet deep and as wide, was completely hidden in a torrent that was heavy and black with silt and going like a mill race out into the valley that drained into the Chin Lee.

A strip of mud more than a half a mile wide crossed the road our freight teams had to come over. One wagon was out there two nights and a day, down to the wagon bed in mud.

We had been so worried about the drought and consequent starvation that we were not so excited as the occasion justified when Mr. Taylor finally started the building of the new store.

A wagonload of Mexicans moved in to put it up. I, who had been considered too tender and delicate to endure the hardships, had spent nearly two years in the old shell of a shack and enjoyed it, but of course I was pleased that we were to have a new building with warehouse in the basement and store and living rooms above.

I quickly appreciated the fact that from the upper windows I would be able to see a full mile along the

trail toward the mountains. I would be able to look out
the window and tell Teddy or Witte that Ken and the
other horse were returning from a long trip.

The Mexicans did not arouse my friendship as the
Indians had done, but if these dark-skinned people —
their skins tended toward the black while the Indians
were more brown — could build an adobe house as sub-
stantial, as cool in summer and as warm in winter as
that at Lugontale, no one would hear any anti-race
comments from me.

The logs Hosteen Nez hauled had been seasoning
months; the freighters had even brought in baled hay
to feed the extra horses; the Mexicans brought scrapers;
the Little Bidoni's teams hauled lumber for the frames
and flooring.

The Mexican family consisted of a man and wife, a
brother of one of them and three children. We did not
speak Mexican and neither did our Indians, so we
couldn't get acquainted much with the newcomers.
Navajos and Mexicans were rarely friendly and those
meeting with us were no exception. The Mexicans pretended not to see the Indians and the Indians stood at a
distance and watched with a curious and unfriendly
scowl.

In the pauses of trade and barter, we watched the new
building grow out of the natural stone and mud and
thought less and less of it. Believing these Mexicans were
poor workmen, Ken finally sent a note to Lugontale
saying as much.

The excavating for the basement was finished. One
day we helped or stood about and watched while the

big spruce poles that were to support the first flooring were put in.

The walls of the first floor were constructed and were four feet thick. If they stood up at all, the house should be warm enough. During the night a wall settled and split the door frame. The Mexicans took some mud and filled in the angle to make the door opening square again, though a few inches smaller. Then they went about putting on the roof logs.

Ken so completely disapproved of the whole thing that he would not even watch but went off on Teddy to see the Little Bidoni's red stallion. He and the Little Bidoni were like two dear friends, and I felt rather left out and wondered how the Indian's three wives felt. I wished I knew them better.

For three days the Mexicans wheeled on dirt in hand barrows and spread it over the new roof. That roof! Tons of dirt over planks laid on twelve-inch spruce logs not entirely dry and placed three feet apart. Ken declared those poorly constructed walls would never stand the weight and forbade me to go inside. Each morning the Mexicans covered with mud the cracks that had come during the night.

The walls were plastered with red sand and would have looked very well to us if we could have forgotten the cracks.

Fritz finished the banister on the stairs and made second-story window frames. How really spacious and civilized it looked. We could be so comfortable there but ——

Because we had been very busy trading all morning,

we sat at lunch late one day. Fritz finished his meal and went back to work. Suddenly there was a crash and a rumbling like rocks in a river bed at freshet time. Ken and I jumped to the door in time to see Fritz take a flying leap from the upper floor and land running, on the hard ground below.

A slow but powerful hand seemed to have gripped that building from the inside. The roof settled, not in one terrible crash, but slowly; the walls of mud and rock crumpled and fell inwards through the flooring; a continuous roar and rumble of falling rock and loose dirt from the roof accompanied the whole settling. The spruce logs stood at last like giant toothpicks in a heaped mud saucer.

Both Mexican men had been on the roof wheeling on more dirt in wheelbarrows when the cave-in started. They got to the outer edge and down unhurt, but both were in tears.

We ran to see if Fritz were hurt. He had made a terrible leap for an old man. At the time he walked to his tent and lay down, but after the excitement was over, he found that an old rupture was hurting him.

The Mexican men, with the woman and children helping them, spent the night sobbing and wailing in their tent.

All of our hopes for some comfort and conveniences were completely buried in that building collapse. The wreck was cleared away; the logs repiled, and some Indians, under Ken's direction, built a roof on the basement wall which was all of stone; the upper story had been all of mud. This gave us more space to store sup-

plies than the whole of the old building and was lovely
and cool besides.

Poor old Fritz had to be sent out to a doctor's care.
Those worthless Mexicans returned to Lugontale to
work out there the debt they owed Mr. Taylor, and
we accepted the prospect of another winter in the old
building.

Hopi Cattle

The fall is cattle-buying season, a busy season for
the Indian trader. Nearly every morning we were
awakened about three-thirty by the knocking of some
wise savage who had ridden by night in order to have
the coolest hours for driving his cattle. Since he arrived
hungry, he thought nothing of pounding on the door
and shouting, "Oh, my brother and sister! Oh, my
grandchildren, your hungry uncle stands at your door,
starving." He was willing to be any relative he thought
we might be happy to see.

At first, when we were so wakened, we tried to
tell our caller we were asleep, we were not going to get
up; but it was no use. Daylight came about three-thirty
or four and those heathen could not understand why
one should be unwilling to be awakened "just before
sunrise." They put in long hours themselves and thought
white men were very lazy about getting up early or
staying up all night. They did both willingly but often
slept in the daytime. I have seen from one to half a
dozen men sound asleep, stretched out on a hogan floor
while the women of the household spoke in whispers

and, as they did their work, stepped carefully over the men.

But I'm off the subject of cattle deals. Three-thirty would start the day for both the Indians and ourselves. When an Indian sold stock, he bought goods.

One particularly busy day Ken was outside buying cattle and I was trying to supply the Navajos' demands inside and at the same time not be cheated out of my eyeteeth.

"I beg your pardon. I know you are very busy, but I should like to speak to you." The voice was just at my elbow and the English was entirely without accent. I would have been less surprised if a ballet dancer had suddenly appeared on the counter before me. The store was full of Utcity's crowd — Utcity himself and sons and sons' wives. The school-going children were, I knew, not at home, so the speaker could be none of my customers.

Before the stranger had said two sentences, the eight or ten in Utcity's crowd were silent. They could not understand English, but they intended to hear, even if they didn't understand.

"We are from the Hopi reservation," the stranger made no attempt to lower his voice, "and we are looking for stolen cattle that were driven from our range about three days ago."

Silence. The Navajo men did not move. The women hid their faces in their shawls and leaned over the counter. The men looked blank and when I noticed that, I realized I was looking blank myself.

There were two Hopis and they were most polite

and quite at ease. The one who did the talking introduced himself and then his companion. The very silence of the Navajos emphasized their unfriendliness, but from the Hopis' manner one would never have guessed that they knew there was an enemy near.

The speaker commented on the weather and the water supply, just as a white man might. I answered as best I could and thought the conversation was getting on safe ground; but the Hopi, still quite at ease, again stated his business. He was as courteous as if some of Utcity's crowd understood; perhaps he thought they did.

"It has happened often that Hopi cattle have strayed into Navajo territory. Recently our losses have been great. We have heard that you were buying stock this fall, so we have come to describe our brands that you may know them and not buy." Suddenly he began to speak in Navajo but did not change his voice or manner the least bit. "With your permission, we will look at the beef hides you have on hand to see if any with our brands are there."

Every Navajo understood that last but there was not a murmur from one of them nor a change in position. Ken came in just then and the Hopi repeated his request. Ken at once led the way to the tent where the dried hides were piled. Several of the Navajo men followed and stood by silently, while Ken and the Hopis lifted every hide, examined the brand carefully and put the hide into another pile. The women in the store did not move, and I could only wait and wonder what would happen if hides from Hopi stock were found. It was as much of a gamble what would happen if no such hides were in our possession.

When every hide had been inspected by eyes that seemed keen enough to count the hairs, the men trailed back to the store. The Hopis thanked Ken and were preparing to go, when old Utcity himself spoke with quiet dignity "The Hopi cattle drink at the Redrock water hole when the season is dry, as now. Since you are so far in the country of the *deneh,* go there also and look at the stock that comes to drink. The Hopi cattle may still wear their skins, even on the range of the *deneh.*"

It was a rebuke and reprimand. The Hopi answered as quietly and in Navajo. "The white man may have bought the hide without question. I accuse no one." Then in English, "This man thinks I am looking for trouble. I hope you folks will understand. My cattle have been run off and stolen. I have lost twenty head this last year; others in my pueblo have lost. We know the Navajos do it but so far we have not caught any one." Then in Navajo, but without change of voice, "I know it is not this man; he now has all the cattle he can take care of, but I do know others that would kill a steer of mine and bring the hide here to sell to you. That is why I am here."

All this was a polite way of telling us that Utcity was stealing Hopi cattle, and the Hopis knew it but couldn't catch him.

Without waiting for us to answer his accusation, the Hopi spoke in Navajo, "We ride to the Redrock water hole. If any doubt our errand, let them follow us."

That whole interview took nerve on the part of the Hopis, but no bit of it took more than the way they said good-by to us, turned their backs on the Navajos, crossed to their waiting horses and without a glance behind rode away to the south into hostile country.

When they were gone, Ken and the Navajos looked from one to the other. For a moment no one moved; then a young man leaned across the counter toward me and began to sing:

"There was a little, little bird
That hid in a bush, in a bush;
And the hawk went by, and the hawk went by
And the little, little bird was safe in the bush;
Quite far, far away he heard the hawk's cry."

At the end of the song every one laughed and cried out happily, as if we had a good joke known only to us.

One of the women who had stood by the counter with her face buried now raised her head and pushed toward Ken a roll of something wrapped in a piece of muslin, as they wrap the blankets they bring in for sale. He unrolled the wrapping and found a fresh steer hide; it was heavy and wet but rolled compactly and tied snugly underneath the muslin.

Every one laughed and the change was like sunshine. Even Ken and I laughed; there seemed to be something really clever in the trick, much as I didn't like the general tone of the whole thing.

Ken said later that it was a brave Hopi who would take the dare to ride to the Redrock water hole, but we heard from the Navajos that that was exactly where our visitors went. Never for a moment of their two days' journey were they unwatched by a Navajo. No one of the *deneh* went within speaking distance, but always on rocky spur or against the sky line was a Navajo who could see the two Hopis and be seen by them.

How thoroughly and intensely these people did things!

Ken explained that there was an old quarrel between Navajos and Hopis and that all the cattle thieves were not on one side. I felt as if we were becoming involved and did not approve of the part we had taken, but we were soon taking even more of a part.

A week after the Hopi visit, we were roused late at night by the same two Hopis. They had a load of wild hay they wanted to sell. We asked them to wait until the next day, but they insisted they must be back on their reservation by daylight. We always needed hay and could never get the Navajos to bring us enough, so we got up at once. By the way the ponies had to pull to get the load to the stack yard, we realized this was a big load. The three men weighed the hay and piled it while I checked weights.

When the last of the hay was out of the wagon, we came to a canvas and under the canvas were eight quarters of excellent beef.

The Hopi said, "We'll weigh this too."

Ken hesitated and in that second's pause he and I both realized that the Hopis were quite well aware of the fact that we had played hand and glove with Utcity's crowd on the occasion of their previous call.

HOPI

How entirely unplanned our part had been the Hopis could never know, but now they took our friendly coöperation as much for granted as the Navajos had done.

Without waiting for directions, they drove to the meat house, Ken and I with them. The meat was weighed and hung up.

"Now," said the Hopis, "we will trade quickly and go."

They did. There was no nickel-by-nickel buying. In less than an hour from the time we had been awakened, the hay and beef had exchanged hands and the Hopis had loaded their wagon with flour, sugar, dress materials and canned goods and were gone.

In the light of a smoky kerosene lamp Ken and I were left standing in the store, looking at each other.

"What would they have done if we hadn't taken the beef?" I asked.

Ken picked up the lamp and led the way to our living room. "I don't know," he said, with his back to me. "They both had guns under their shirts."

I hadn't realized this was true. Would they have used them? The whole transaction had seemed so friendly, almost jovial.

The next day the Navajos saw the fresh meat through the screen windows of the meat house. They asked whose steers we had bought and when we butchered them. Ken replied that he had bought the meat ready dressed but did not say from whom.

In two hours a dozen Navajos had arrived and were following Ken around, begging him to tell where he got the beef. Ken's only answer was that he had bought and paid for it. They asked to see our pile of hides and of course found no fresh ones. That convinced them that the steers really had not been killed in our corral. At once one fellow began looking for tracks.

In no time, it seemed, he was back with the solution. A wagon and team had come in from the north and had gone back the same way. The pace had been fast both ways, but faster going back. The Navajos gave themselves to several days of hard riding to learn who among them had lost two steers.

Ken teased them about the deal and they took it as a good joke on themselves. For a couple of weeks, when they smelled steak cooking on the stove, they would sniff, hold their heads on one side, look knowing and say to me, "Is San Chee cooking Hopi beef or *deneh* beef?" Then they'd laugh.

Some traders absolutely refused to buy either sheep or cattle from Navajos. Two Englishmen had a trading post some fifteen miles from us. We saw very little of them as their road went out on the other side and the trail between us was of the roughest. However, at the beginning of the cattle-buying season that fall of 1916, one of them did ride over with a Navajo guide to ask if we would drive out with our herd the cattle he had bought — twelve head.

Ken agreed to take the extras provided they were delivered at our corral. He asked the Englishman what Indians he had bought from and what the brands on the cattle were.

"I don't know the brands — Indian brands are so

peculiar I can't remember them," was the answer, "and the Navajo names, — who could spell them? I have them down in my book as Jones and Smith and Brown."

Truly here was a business deal. He could identify the Indians by those names but no one else could; he didn't know a brand and could not describe minutely the animals he had bought. But his guide here had sold him two steers.

Ken turned to the guide, who was Cla's youngest brother. That heathen grinned and told Ken the two steers we had bought, butchered and sent to an Indian school a week previously were the same two steers. He was as proud and pleased as could be. The Englishman looked dumbfounded. Such things were not in his code.

"Has this man any silver pawned with you?" Ken asked.

The Englishman nodded. "A silver bridle, a belt and some other things."

"Keep them until he pays you the value of those steers," Ken suggested.

Of course not one of the steers the Britisher had paid for was driven in to our corral, to go out with our herd and he vowed he would never again buy a sheep or a cow from a Navajo. This very greatly decreased his trade.

Ken spent all the time he could riding the range with the Indians. He knew every brand and, most amazing of wonders to me, he remembered not only the brand on the animal he had contracted for; but, what was more important, because some Indian cattle are not branded and some are so scarred the brand cannot be identified, he remembered the exact spots on the animals. If an Indian did not bring in a steer Ken had agreed to take, Ken went after it, brought it in, and added the price of delivery to whatever pawn we were holding for that particular Navajo.

Chindi (Devils) — and Pottery

It was in November or December, 1916, a mild warm day for the season, that I walked as I nearly always did, when I had a little time outside the store, to the hogans of the Old Lady and her married daughters, Slender Girl and Robert's second wife. On the way I picked up some bits of pottery. Old they were, surely.

Showing the bits to the Old Lady, I said, "I wish I could find a bowl like these."

Both the Old Lady and Slender Girl looked up from the blanket they were working on together.

"Come," smiled Slender Girl. She showed me a mound covered with broken bits of the pottery.

In one place the wind had blown the sand and dirt away and a bone was exposed to view. I tried to pull it out but could not, so I took a splintered piece of bone that lay there and began to dig. Slender Girl shuddered and laughed and squealed at the same time. "It's a devil, maybe," she said, and with that idea in mind, she herded the children back to the hogan.

I dug awkwardly with the shin bone and at last shook the skull and a joint or two of backbone loose from the sand. I missed the lower jaw.

HOPI

I asked if it would be all right for me to bring a shovel and dig, to see if I could find a bowl. The Old Man remarked doubtfully, *"Nee la."* That meant "suit yourself"; but he warned me to keep the skull out of sight and I noticed he would not look directly at it himself. He walked back to the store with me, so I put it in my apron to protect him and others. He told me a pregnant woman would die if she looked at it.

Ken laughed and said I might have to move a train-load of dirt, but back I went the next day. Slender Girl followed and even helped to dig a little, as long as no bones were in sight, but kept the children in the hogan. I found the lower jawbone of the skull I had dug out the day before, a bone awl and a tanning stone. Then there was nothing but dirt, until it was too dark to see.

Even Ken was pleased and a little impressed by what I had found, but he still thought that the rain and snow that set in the next morning saved me useless work.

The very day the drizzle stopped, I dragged him out of the tent where he was baling hides and planted him behind the counter in the store, with orders to stay there until I got back.

He hoped the ground would be so wet I couldn't dig, but I didn't need to dig. In the side of the hole I had made I could see the curved surface of a jar or bowl. The storm had washed off the last pinch of dirt. I shuddered! What if in my work I had thrust the shovel through it!

I sat down and dug with my hands and a stick. Not until I had a crude black jar of a primitive basket pat-

tern in my hands did I remember I had promised Ken
I would not be gone more than an hour.

With the jar in my apron for its safety, rather than
for the protection of the neighbors, I hurried back over
the wet trail.

I had never seen Ken more pleased. "Earlier than the
Cliff Dwellers, sure enough," he said, as his hands
brushed the rough surface. I stayed in the store then;
but instead of going back to the hides, he put up in
our living room a shelf with a protecting cleat across
the front; and we had a really precious possession.

Narcissus

Another important event of the winter months of
1916–1917 was the arrival of some narcissus bulbs.
The year before I had bulbs in window boxes but for
all my nursing only a few hyacinths and daffodils
bloomed. I dried the bulbs carefully, put them away —
and let them freeze. Ken discovered this bit of domestic
tragedy only a few days before the arrival of the
narcissus bulbs.

At once we put them in a large-sized oval sardine
can and surrounded them with our own brand of
Black Mountain alkali water and some bright and
nourishing chips of petrified wood.

At night we put the dish and two warm flatirons in
a large coffee can and wrapped an old blanket around
all. At once our chief pastime became a contest as to
whether Ken or I should be the first to see a new point
of green or bit of root.

HOPI

The Navajos asked if the bulbs were onions and if we were going to eat them.

The flowers had not appeared when we became involved in widespread disaster, forgot the plants and let them freeze.

XIV · THE SICKNESS WITH
THE SORES

I NEVER should have supposed I could be calm in a smallpox epidemic. It came upon us suddenly and almost immediately dozens of our friends and customers were dead.

The Indians came to the post with their bodies covered with sores; they lay down on the floor beside the stove, sick as could be, unable to climb on their ponies again and go home.

The weather was raw and cold and wet and our stove was red hot; some one was stoking it with pitchy piñon wood every few moments. After our floor, the camp hogan was the next resting place. From there some relative would help the sick person into a wagon or onto his pony and get him home to die. The odor of wet clothes and the feverish steaming eruption combined left an everlasting memory.

It was not the least use for Ken and me to be careful; the disease was everywhere. Of course, when a medicine man treated anyone, a crowd came to the ceremony and the disease was spread more effectually.

Hosteen Nez, whom I had scarcely seen since he cut the house poles and had fed White Hat and myself at his hogan, came in, looking thin and haggard. I hardly knew him; and when I took his proffered hand, I felt the pox sores in my palm and turned him toward the light to look better into his face. He was covered with smallpox eruption. He smiled weakly and told me that he was getting better but that two of his children had died and that the others in his hogan were sick. He had come for food; the medicine man was at his hogan and they hoped to save the rest of the family.

Of course, I took his money and pawned his beads, though there must have been enough germs on them to have destroyed a nation.

Such things were of daily occurrence. Vaccination had been explained to the Indians years ago by government agents and outbreaks of smallpox among the Mexicans had spread to the reservation before. Many of the Navajos hurried to the agencies to be vaccinated, but the sickness spread so quickly that hundreds did not have time to get there before they or their families were down.

The agency doctor at Chin Lee sent me vaccine, in order that I could immunize those who came to us and so save them the twenty-mile journey to Chin Lee.

It was getting dark early on one of our hardest, most trying days, when Slender Girl came close to me in the doorway, her shawl drawn high around her head so that I did not see her face. She clung to my hands and bent her forehead until it rested on my shoulder and stood still. A great fear gripped my heart.

Ken saw us standing there and stopped suddenly on his way to the tent with an armful of goatskins. He was tired with much trade and the distress and suffering of our friends, "What, who now?" he asked. I shook my head. "She has not told me yet. I'm afraid to have her," I said and waited. A long quivering sob came from Slender Girl and she raised her head and whispered, "My mother — the sores — help us."

"It's the Old Lady," I cried. "Ken, what shall I do?"

Ken stood still. "But she was vaccinated with the others, wasn't she?"

"No, no," I could hardly speak. "She insisted that all the rest be done first; there was not enough vaccine. She is the only one in the family who was not vaccinated."

Ken dropped the goathides and turned to the shelves; he piled canned goods and calico on Slender Girl's shawl and I went with her to help carry the things and to see if I could do anything to help our friend.

The Old Lady lay quietly on her bed of pelts; her fever was high; I hardly knew her; I urged water. She nodded and promised to drink often and I could only go home again. It was almost noon when word came to us that the Old Lady was dead.

Hosteen Blue Goat, her father, wept on my shoulder

and said, "Oh, my friend, her children will be hungry, her loom will be empty, her hogans will never be happy as they were; she called you her child; she loved you; you will feed her children."

I promised to do all I could and sent a new granite pan for the grave.

The few blankets of the Old Lady's weaving that we had became treasures and mementos, and the work of a genius and an artist. I tried to express some of this to Slender Girl and Robert's young wife, and urged them both to remember the old patterns and keep up the fine record for beautiful work that their mother had established. Slender Girl said, "We have her weaving sticks; we have her loom frame; we have her sheep. Her work will go on."

Ken sent word to the Utcity hogans, urging them to bring every one, in wagons if necessary, for vaccination, and in a few days they came in wagons, in buggy and on horseback.

The smallest, a boy about four years old, had never been to a store before, his father told us. The others, one girl and three boys, were all shy and sweet and unusually well dressed. They all had on silver belts and beads. The little girl, who was about fourteen, must have had on six pounds of silver, including the lovely blue turquoise ear loops of fine beads which announced she was of marriageable age.

My apparatus and technique for vaccination consisted of soap and water to wash a clean spot on the arm, then the scraping of a small area and the rubbing in of a small drop of vaccine.

245

DESERT WIFE

In this instance Ken and the Little Bidoni stood leaning against the high counter in the store, while I arranged my things on the counter. The Little Bidoni stood where he could see the members of his family being vaccinated, but he did not show a wrinkle of anxiety. The children and the three wives, as I vaccinated them, never for a moment took their eyes from the Little Bidoni's face; he gave them very quiet, straight looks but seemed to be engaged with the conversation which he and Ken carried on by unspoken agreement.

Ken: You have a large and handsome family, my friend.

L. B.: Oh, yes. I am happy that you say so. My family is happy at the hogans.

Ken: Your girl is very beautiful. She is quiet and well-behaved like her mother, who makes the fine blankets.

L. B.: Yes, you are right. My daughter is a good girl. She owns many sheep and is going to be wise like her mother.

Ken: My friend, your boys are all brave and strong.

L. B.: La-a-a, my brother. My sons, as you see, are all brave. Not one would flinch from any small pain.

Just here I was vaccinating the four-year-old boy. He was as white as a brown skin could be but made no sound or movement.

Ken: You speak truly. Your sons are all brave and unafraid. I know that all your sons will be fine *deneh*.

L. B.: My boys will all stand pain, — all, from my eldest who is a grown man, to my youngest who is here with us now. He is no longer a baby who might be afraid but a brave son to make me proud, because he is like his brothers, strong and without fear.

Ken: Now I see why you are a happy father. Your sons are all brave and unafraid. It is truly good. Please allow my wife, who likes brave boys, to fill a bag with candy for each of your children who is here to-day.

My wife gives this strong medicine to many of the *deneh*. They come every day for it, because they do not want to be sick with the sores. Even little children come for the medicine. The brave ones, like your boys here, for instance, do not mind. What, all done? *A-la-hon-i.* Done so soon. Now for the candy.

So I put the candy and cookies in paper bags and they all went away happy. The Little Bidoni was very proud that none of his children had been frightened at what must have been an ordeal for them.

A week later the government doctor at Chin Lee ran out of vaccine. We simply had to have some so I started to the railroad for it.

I have a sinking feeling whenever I think of that seven days. A circuit of one hundred and seventy-five miles with a Navajo team and the Navajo. Snow! Drifts! Mud! Slow travel!

I did not suppose anything in this world would justify to me the whipping of a horse, but that Navajo team was the most aggravating thing that ever existed. As I left the post at four in the morning, Ken said, "Don't let him drive hard until afternoon. Take it easy until the horses get strung out."

Don't let him drive hard! By whipping, yelling and

slashing, we could get that team to trot — downhill — never otherwise. If for two minutes the driver stopped his belaboring, the team stopped. He would stand up, lean over the dashboard and lash with all his might, and the horses would walk slowly out of the road and come to a dead standstill; he'd pull on the line to turn them back and they'd twist their necks, open their mouths and stand there. Several times he had to get out and slash them around the legs and shoo them back into the road as he would an old cow.

The wonder to me was that not once did that Indian appear to lose his temper; he didn't seem to think he was passing through anything unusual. For a while I was fairly sick with the whipping, and then I regretted I hadn't brought a pitchfork.

At noon we stopped at a water hole, fed those beasts and ate our own lunch. One horse would not eat corn, had never learned to like it. Many Indian ponies will not eat grain of any kind, even when they are starving. At first, I thought the horse was worn out and too tired to eat, and I began to feel remorse for wanting that pitchfork; but when the Indian tried to catch the brute to hitch up — and the beast hobbled too — I got over my pity and remorse.

We got under way again with twenty miles, mostly upgrade, to go. I can't tell about the first eleven miles. Sometimes I think I am still traveling that road and always will. It was endless. When nine miles from Lugontale, our destination the first day, we came to the Keams Canyon road. For five miles that led across a wide valley. Five miles of mud and melting snow!

Hard footing for any team — but for that one! We crept and slid and staggered so slowly that when we stopped, as we often did, it would be several seconds before I realized we were standing still. It was sundown. Still miles of mud ahead of us and the horses done out. A cold night was coming and I began to wonder if I could make it the rest of the way on foot in the moonlight. Again, I thought it would be wiser to wait until the mud began to freeze and we could travel better.

I had not decided, when the mail from Keams, two men in a light rig, passed us. They stopped when they could look back into our top buggy and see the passengers were not all Indians. One of the men insisted that he and I change seats, so I could get to the stopping place before night. I agreed and waded in mud over my shoe tops to make the change. Rejoicing to have mud splattered on me by a real live team, away I went.

My Indian got in at ten o'clock, his passenger an hour earlier, because he got out and walked.

It snowed that night and we had a blizzard for the next two days. The road to Gallup was so bad that every one advised me not to try it. Finally one of the men at Lugontale volunteered to go and I let him. Hoping the road would be better, my Navajo and I went back by Nozlini and Chin Lee. It was a little farther but there were two places to stop instead of one.

So ended my travels. I vowed I'd not go out again until I could go in an airship.

Gradually the plague passed and we heard of no

more deaths or new cases. It was like waking from a nightmare to find that the worst of it had really happened. Ken was tired and more than ever silent; he stayed at the post more and rode less. We were grateful for the work that kept us too busy to think always of those who no longer came to the store.

XV · GUARDED GOLD

ONE afternoon we were trading with our friends, the Old Buzzard and two of her worthless sons, all of whom came to trade out a blanket made by one son's wife. The Old Buzzard herself brought me another clay cooking jar — she always did.

The door opened and a newcomer, a man I had never seen before, fine-looking and alert, a true blanket Indian, stepped inside. He stood beside the stove for a few moments, warming himself. The others grunted and clasped his hand shortly. Ken and Cla Nez were back in the ware tent, weighing a horsehide.

The stranger came to me and I reached across the counter to take his hand. "You come from far off," I said. "I do not know you."

"Yes," he answered, waving his hand to the north; "I live a long, long way, but I have been on the Black Mountain and heard that the white woman at this store gave the strong medicine in the arm which prevents the sickness that kills. I came to see if I could have some of that medicine. I have been many days and nights with *deneh* who have the sickness. I thought I did not want to be like that; I would go for the medicine. Then my friends say, 'Go to the Covered Water trading post; the white woman at that place has made all our arms sore for us and we have not had the killing sickness — so I came."

Of course, I was pleased and promised to make his arm sore for him just as soon as my husband came back from weighing a horsehide.

The stranger leaned against the counter and rolled a cigarette. I passed more matches. The Old Buzzard did not know that I had seen her take all there were in the stone bowl.

Ken and Cla came into the store and Ken turned to open the picket gate that led behind the counter, as he called to me, "Allow him three dollars for his horsehide and give him the bracelet he left here a year ago."

There was an astonished gasp from the stranger. "*A la hootsa, sekiss, sekiss hoskay-da.*" (Ah, my friend, my friend of long ago.) Ken whirled about and for moments the rest of us just stared.

Those two grown men seized each other by the shoulders; they stamped their feet and shouted endearing names at each other. I did not know that Ken could show so much joy over anything. They were so glad to see each other that they kept saying so over and over, and there were so many "Do you remembers" that I could not tell all they did say; but mostly the talk seemed to be about the times that they had shot wild turkeys together or had driven six bronchos on a freight wagon to Gallup and back — all this years ago when Ken had been an Indian trader on the east slope of the mountains.

I went for my basin and vaccine, and while they talked I made the fellow's arm sore. He thanked me for it; then he and Ken had cookies and ginger ale together; others came in and in another hour the men were all out in front of the store, shooting at a tomato can on a stump.

At the first firing, Lady Betty fled to her box, growling savagely and carrying two cookies with her. The Old Buzzard decided on tomatoes, after all, gathered up her things and left; but her two sons stayed. They pawned their bracelets again to buy cartridges and joined the target shooting.

I was left alone and took the opportunity to go into the kitchen and get supper. It was too dark to see the sights on a gun before the shooting stopped. Of course, the noise of the shooting had brought in every Indian within six miles; there had been betting and the winners, Ken and his friend, had to treat the crowd. They all sat about on the floor with red paper boxes of soda crackers, cans of peaches and pears opened before them, and each man with a spoon. I made coffee, and our visitors were just like any group of tired happy men after a good trap-shooting contest.

Soon they began telling stories of like shootings. As I listened, I gathered that they all respected the stranger, Hosteen Tsay-nez; he was famous for straight shooting and great nerve.

One of the others turned to me and said, "This man Tsay-nez is very brave; years ago it was given to him to shoot the white men who came here to rob the *deneh*. It has been his work to keep all white men from going to the place where the gold is in the ground. Your man knows; he has heard; ask him to tell you the story."

They all nodded, Ken too; and one, speaking slowly, reminded the others, "It is years now since any white man has tried to find the place — it is forgotten now among the white men, maybe."

"Yes," another spoke as slowly. "Perhaps now the white men have all the gold they want; certainly they have plenty when they charge five dollars for a sack of flour and will pay three dollars for a poor horsehide."

"But I do not know this story," I said. "Tell me, what place, what gold. I have not heard."

"It was long ago; twenty years, perhaps more; shall I tell the tale?" To-Clazin looked around him. All there, I think, knew the tale except myself; nevertheless, they all urged, "Tell — tell. It is long since we have heard."

It passed through my mind that here was a thing that Ken had known all the time and might have told me long ago. It was a strange group: the men sitting quite comfortably on the floor; the cracker

boxes, and the empty cans with the spoons in them
set aside. Some one got up and, taking the stone tobacco
bowl from the counter, placed it on the floor. Every
Indian reached for his corn-husk cigarette papers. Ken
never smoked. The air was soon blue. I sat on the
counter, looking down on them; some one opened the
stove door; the piñon and cedar sticks snapped and
blazed inside.

It was To-Clazin who told the story; he had heard
the shooting and, thinking we must be butchering
many beeves, had almost ridden his pony down to get
to the post; then he stayed to play with the rest.

"As I say," he began again, "it was maybe twenty-
five years ago when we were all younger than we are
now, and our horses were stronger and carried us all
day without tiring so much as my pinto did to-day,
in only a few miles.

"White men did not often come here; trading posts
were a long day's ride apart, often more. Then one
time two white men came, not to trade. They carried
little to eat; they had mules and big strong horses,
and they had shovels and picks, steel bars and heavy
hammers on the mules.

"The *deneh* who saw them did not understand why
they came. It was years since soldiers had been here,
but these were not soldiers or traders; so one of the
deneh went to old Hoskinene the wise, Hoskinene who
lived near by the moon-water place, and he described
to him the things that these two white men carried;
and old Hoskinene said, 'Watch them. Do not lose
sight of them. They are looking for gold. I have seen

those tools among white men. They dig in the rocks with them.'

"We watched the two white men and after a time they went into the hills and climbed about among the rocks and worked very hard in one place, and after a few days they loaded some heavy canvas sacks which they carried with bits of rock that they had broken up. These sacks they put on the mules and went away, riding fast and whipping their horses and mules to make them hurry. Some of us followed at a distance; and one we sent back to Hoskinene so he should know, for he was very wise.

"On the night that these two white men and their mules and horses camped in the big place where the square rocks stand high against the sky ——— "

Here Ken put in for my information, "He means Monumental Valley."

"On that night it was that Hoskinene rode alone to talk with the white men; he rode to their camp; he carried no gun. By signs he made them understand that he would show them water for their horses and mules, which were very dry and thirsty; he rode with them to the spring near the fluted red butte; he watered their mules and helped to take the packs off; he felt of the heavy bags and asked what the rocks were for. The men took money from their pockets and by signs said that both were the same; they gave Hoskinene the money and put the rock back into the sack and tied it up again; they laughed a great deal and patted Hoskinene on the back and held his hand; they were like crazy men.

"Then they ate and offered food to Hoskinene, but he thanked them and, sitting apart from them, he ate the dried meat he carried with him. The white men lay down in their blankets and went to sleep. Hoskinene lay down and waited. After a time he got up and, taking the white men's ax, he struck one and then the other on the head; and they lay still. He took the heavy sacks and emptied out the stones up against the butte and covered the place with other stones. He drove the white men's horses and mules away for several miles and shot them all with the white men's guns. It was hard for Hoskinene; and he rode away from that place until he came to where the *deneh* were, and they had new word for him."

To-Clazin paused and leisurely finished his cigarette. The others stirred a little, but waited without speaking.

"Hoskinene listened to the new word. It was this. More white men were coming, seven more; they were riding fast and carried shovels and picks and very little food. They were one day's ride away on the trail of the first two white men. Again Hoskinene the wise told us what to do and we did it.

"At night, when the seven white men camped, we came forward in a large circle and built small fires which we fed slowly with bits of brush that we carried. In the darkness the white men saw the little fires making a ring all about them, and when daylight came they could see us, sixty of us, on horses in a ring around them. The white men did not try to move camp that day and the next night it was the same.

They had water in canteens but their horses had none. Some of the horses the white men held with ropes. A few got away from them and we did not stop their going. They came to our line and we let them through.

"On the second day one of the white men walked out and called us. It was Tsay-nez here who went to talk to him. The white man said, 'What do you want with us?' And Tsay-nez answered, 'Nothing at all; this is our country; what do you want here?' The white man replied, 'Two other white men came this way; we are looking for them.' And Tsay-nez asked, 'Why do you carry picks and shovels and strong canvas bags, if you seek only your friends?'

"Then the white man seemed to be worried and he said, 'Take us to where these two white men are and we will pay you money' — and Tsay-nez told him, 'They are one day's ride from this place and are waiting until you come. Bring one other man with you and I will show you the place. They are dead.'

"The white man looked very hard at Tsay-nez. 'This will go hard with you; you know there are many white men and only a few Navajos. Why did you do this thing?'

"And Tsay-nez said, 'Go and bring the wisest among you. I will take you to the place; you may bury your friends, but neither they nor you may take the heavy stones away in the strong canvas bags.'

"The white man turned to go for his friend and again Tsay-nez spoke to him, 'Neither of you may bring a gun; you will not be hurt; we only take you to bury your friends and the shovels are near them now.'

"The white man said, 'Yes', and after a long time he and one other came on horses. We searched them but they had no guns. Five white men remained for the others to watch, and Hoskinene and Tsay-nez rode with the two white men to the place where the dead ones lay. The white men worked very hard and dug places in the sand near the rock slide from the fluted butte and there, without unrolling them from their blankets, they buried the two dead men and piled many big stones over the place; they made two large, pointed piles of rock that can be seen from far off even now, and this was many years ago.

"Then the two white men, looking about the camp, picked up one of the strong canvas bags that Hoskinene had emptied, and they shook it and picked up little pinches of the sand and broken pieces that stayed in the bag; they talked long and asked if they might have the empty sacks with the other things that belonged to the two dead men.

"Because it is not good to keep the property of the dead among us, Hoskinene advised that they leave all things beside the stone piles; but they asked again for the bags, after they had placed all the shovels and picks and cooking pans beside the graves, as was proper; so they kept the empty bags and the four rode together back to the place where the little fires were in a circle; and we let them through and heard the two white men talking fast and in excitement to the five white men.

"Before daylight came Hoskinene and Tsay-nez gave more good counsel and we put out the little fires to the north and waited. After a time we could hear the white men moving, and we moved back, leaving the way to the north free and open. The white men passed one behind the other with their mules and horses. They rode slowly but very straight. We followed them at each side and behind them. Daylight came and we rode, keeping always in sight. They rode steadily and did not speak to any of us again, and we stayed farther and farther behind. When they came to the reservation line, which is the river, we watched them cross and rode back to our hogans.

"It was then that Hoskinene told us that the white men must never be allowed to take the heavy stones from the country of the *deneh*, that the place where they were should be guarded and any white man who tried to go there should be killed.

"For a while we feared that soldiers would come against us and we were ready for them; but none came and a year passed. Then three of the seven white men came back and it was Tsay-nez who met them, and they did not find the place they sought.

"So it has been ever since. No white man has reached the place where the valuable stones are; but five of the seven who were surrounded by the little fires came back, three together, as I have said, then one alone, then two; they were brave men, all. They stayed. Tsay-nez met them and none went away again.

"In all these years we have learned that white men call this rock gold and value it above everything, even

"No white man has reached the place where the valuable stones are; . . ."

their lives. The *deneh,* our people, must keep this country clear and free for our homes and our sheep. The white men must never find this place where the gold is or they would rob us of the land. It has been explained to me that this could be done and the Indians would be unable to defend themselves; even white men who are our friends agree that this is so."

"It is the truth, it is the truth; often have we heard it; it is all true."

Every one looked satisfied and nodded to his neighbor. I was fairly floored by the story. "And you tell me that the *deneh* in the last twenty-five years have killed seven white men and no one has been here to say who shall hang for this?"

Tsay-nez answered me, "The first two white men came only to take what was not theirs; their one hope was that other white men should not know — and the five who came, three together, and one, and two — they were of the seven who sat in the circle of little fires. They came back to steal, to take what they knew was guarded. They never went back to their homes again. Now we hope that the gold is forgotten — there are two left who know, if they still live — but it is long now. Perhaps they are too wise to come; perhaps they are already dead; who knows?"

I was silent. The rest sat and smoked. To think that this little group of friendly benighted heathen had done this thing red-handed and could tell it and discuss it with such righteousness and satisfaction! They felt they were right and somehow I agreed with them, in spite of myself. *"A-la-honi,"* said one. "The story is told. This white man remembers; he was always our friend; we are his friends. *A-la-honi,* now I go home to my hogan. Who rides towards the west with me?"

Our guests stood up, stretched, moved outside. The moon was high and full. With the smoke-filled room behind me, I stood on the platform, watched the men ride out of sight over the hills and listened to the riding song, floating back from all directions. As I turned, Ken was picking up the empty cans and cracker boxes.

"It's strange," I said, as I went back to help, "that in all the years we've been married you have never told me that. We've been months here on the reservation. It's queer you did not tell me."

"Not queer at all," he answered.

"Are they like that?" I wondered, as the last notes of the song reached us; "or are they murderers, our enemies, perhaps?"

Ken closed the door and blew out the flickering lamp. "Dead men tell no tales and they know it," he said. "They were defending their homes. You can see they think they were right."

I thought of the dead killed in the war and wondered what right I had to moralize over the Indians. They looked at war photographs of men killed with worse than an ax or gun. Perhaps they understood what they saw better than I did. Who was I to tell them white men were better than they or had different rights in defending their homes?

GUARDED GOLD

The Prospector

We had not seen a white man for six months when unexpectedly one afternoon in August, 1917, one rode up to the store. An Indian called, "A white man with a pack mule is here. Come see what he wants." Even on the outside edge of the world where we were, the war was affecting what we did. We must sell corn meal with flour even when the Indians ground their own corn meal. I expected this man to bring some new regulations of our sales, or perhaps he was interested in hides or wool. But the first thing that caught my eye was a prospector's pick across the top of his pack. Every Indian in sight, and there were more of them than usual, looked as dumb as a blank wall. A wave of chill crept up my spine.

The man leaned from his horse and held out his hand. "My name is Derrill," he said "I hope I can buy some feed for my horse and camp by your store to-night."

I assured him he could and that my husband would be back very soon. I showed him where to find the hay and while he made his camp I turned, thinking to send an Indian out in the hope of meeting Ken and telling him to hurry. As I looked about for a messenger, I counted just five Navajos quirting their ponies out of sight over five different trails. There were several left and, calling one aside — it was Nez-Chilly Begay — I said, "Will they find Ken or are they going for the *deneh*?" He looked blank. We were standing perhaps twenty feet from where Mr. Derrill whistled as he fed his horses. I added, "I know the old story. Are they going for Tsay-nez?"

At that Nez-Chilly Begay flashed me the keenest look and said quickly, "They have gone for the *deneh*."

"Then you ride fast and tell Ken to hurry; there must be no trouble here."

He looked at me and said slowly, "There will be no trouble — here."

Just then Mr. Derrill came up, all frankness and good will. I took him inside and as it was nearing sundown, I started supper while we talked.

He was from Texas. I had known he was no tenderfoot. He asked if we had been in the country long and I said, "Oh, yes, ages."

"Well this is my first trip here," he told me. "Years ago, an older brother of mine was in this country and discovered some mighty good gold ore. The Indians got him but the story of the gold got out and has been a sort of tradition in the family ever since. One of the two men whom the Indians guided in to bury my brother and his partner came back to Texas years afterwards and told us all about it. The Indians were really dangerous in those days. I was just a little shaver at the time but I remember the story well. The man drew a map so we could find the place where the graves were. It seems that my brother and his partner were killed within a day's ride of the gold, but in which direction from the mine I don't know. I've promised myself for years that some day I'd come up to this part of the country and look around."

I felt suffocated but tried to appear normal and

hospitable. I could feel the Indians outside; I knew they would not leave; I was sure there were more coming at that very moment.

Mr. Derrill was rambling on good-naturedly. "Yes, I guess the Navajos used to be pretty tricky; it was all a man's life was worth to knock around here, even twenty years ago. A man wouldn't bring a woman out to the jumping-off place like this in those times, you bet. I can see things are different now or you just wouldn't be here at all, let alone staying here and running the store with him riding off somewhere after cattle."

While I was trying to register that secure feeling for Mr. Derrill's benefit, Ken came in; and he had plenty of company, just as I expected.

I introduced the two men and we sat down at once to supper. It was dark outside, but from my seat at table I could look out of the window and see a shower of sparks pouring from the smoke hole of the camp hogan. A few Indians sat quietly in the store, where a lamp burned. I looked them over and, thinking Mr. Derrill might feel more free to talk, remarked, "None of these speak or understand English."

"Yes," Mr. Derrill saw only the surface meaning of my remark. "I can see that I may have difficulty finding an interpreter," he went on to Ken. "The only direction I have to go by is the location of what is called Monumental Valley, which is about sixty miles farther than we are here, I should judge. I figure you can tell me the best way to get there from here?"

"I wish you'd tell my husband just what you told

me," I tried to speak carelessly. "He has been in this country a long time and knows a great deal about places and people here."

Ken listened until the man was through speaking. The Indians outside were as quiet as he was for a long time. Then he said slowly, "You have the right direction for Monumental Valley; you have the outfit to stay a month and prospect for gold that you are not at all sure of finding. A day's ride in any direction from your brother's grave is a big order. You might have to make a dozen trips."

"Yes, I expect to take a lot of time; but I've prospected some in my day, and I can get an idea from the formation which direction I'd want to look over most closely. I'd like to get an early start in the morning. The Indians seem friendly. One tried to buy my pick yesterday, and he brought me all the way out here, when what I wanted was to go to Chin Lee; but he insisted that there was a short way across the mountain here. At least, that is what I understood by his signs; so I came along."

As I understood more clearly myself, the darkness outside became more tensely hostile.

"Well," Ken began, picking his words slowly, "I'm not a prospector; but I do know these Indians a little and I think they feel about the way they always have concerning gold seekers; they never have encouraged prospectors, as you will admit. If there's gold here, no white man will get away with it, alive; if there isn't any gold, you could ride all over the reservation; but what's the use?"

GUARDED GOLD

Mr. Derrill was quite unimpressed by Ken's serious-
ness. "Oh, sure, sure, I see your viewpoint," he said
tolerantly; "but you traders are not looking for a big
stake. You came here to trade and that's what you do.
That's good in its way. Now I've got no particular
hard feelings against these Navajos. The ones that killed
my brother are likely dead long ago. But gold's gold,
you know; and from the stories that came back in the
old days, that ore was so rich that the dust in the
bottom of the sacks, after the Indians had thrown away
the rock itself, was worth something like fifty dollars.
Now I figure if I can find that place and get one good
mule load of ore out, I won't need to come back. I'm
no hog; I don't care about taking the land away from
the poor Injuns nor anything like that, but I do think,
considering they got my brother like they did, that
I've got a little return coming; and I think I'll try to
collect."

Ken's expression never changed at the stranger's
apparently unintended disparagement of Indian traders.
He spoke even more slowly but as if he had thoroughly
made up his mind to talk. "These Indians have not
forgotten that white men have looked for and found
gold in Navajo country. We traders are safe only so
long as we make no move to prospect.

"Your brother and his friend came and found gold
before they were killed. Others came but did not find
gold. They didn't live long enough. Now I know these
Indians. They mean what they say about this gold and
their actions speak louder than I can. I advise you to
get off of this reservation — now. They have your

prospecting tools spotted. You'll never reach gold."

Mr. Derrill looked hard at Ken's serious face. Then he laughed shortly. "Well, I must say you take these fellows more seriously than I do. In Texas we don't let those things bother us. It won't hurt my feelings a lot if I have to pot one or two of these Injuns but I don't expect to start anything. I'm going to jog along about my own business and like as not I won't see a redskin all the way. In fact, this fellow who brought me here is the only one I've seen close since I left Gallup, three days ago, and I've been in Injun country all the way. Now don't think I don't appreciate your warning me, but I'm going on just the same. I'll look around in the Monumental Valley country and go out south to Flagstaff. I'll drop you a card from there and let you know how I make it."

Ken looked the man over slowly. "You are in a country you don't know, among people who are strangers to you. Better try to see their view of things. No white man will take gold from the Derrill and Andrew mine. These Indians guard it and they will kill you without hesitation, even though you get a few of them first. Again I advise you to think it over. Go back to Gallup. They will not touch you if you ride east. One white man more or less makes no difference to a Navajo. We were never popular with them, anyway. They call me friend now; but if I rode with you, they would shoot me as unhesitatingly as they will you. Better not go."

Listening to all this, I wondered that Ken could talk so earnestly and so well, when he habitually talked so little; but Mr. Derrill only shook his head and repeated, "Thanks for the tip; I'll go on and take a look over the land and be out by Flagstaff and away before these fellows know I'm in the country."

"Wait a minute," Ken interrupted him. "Let's see how many of these fellows know you're in the country already. Come outside with me."

They got up and went to the store door. A white moonlight showed ponies tied to every tree and half a dozen little fires and camps scattered about. The scene increased my apprehension. Mr. Derrill looked and said, "They naturally come to a store; your trade must be good."

"You are not even taking a risk," Ken pointed out. "The result is already a certainty."

After all this, I could only admire Mr. Derrill's courage and fearlessness as he left us at the door and went to his camp beside the corral fence. "Good night," he said. "I know you intend this all for my good and I sure do thank you for telling me; but I have not looked forward to this all my life to turn back, now I'm within sixty miles of the place. I can use a pack load of that gold dust and I'm going after it."

He went out into the still white night. Ken stood a minute looking out and then turned back into the house. During the night I could tell by his careful breathing that he did not sleep. If he knew that I was awake, he made no sign.

At dawn when we looked out, Mr. Derrill had gone, — and not a Navajo was in sight.

For the two days after Mr. Derrill's visit Ken did

not ride. He acted as if he expected some one. I was glad somehow that I was not alone at the store. The two days passed, days when the Indians traded and ate canned tomatoes and crackers. About noon of the third day a boy of sixteen, the son of Hosteen Nez, who had come to us for help when his father and mother were stricken with smallpox, and who often came to us for food now that they were gone, asked for crackers and tomatoes. I added a piece of meat from our own table, but he seemed almost too tired to eat. He leaned heavily on the counter, thus bringing his head almost on a level with Ken's, as he stooped to lift a sack of flour.

"Cla and others come to kill you," he whispered.

Ken placed the flour where he could reach it easily and stooped again.

The boy whispered, "The older men do not know that Cla is coming."

There were other Indians in the store, — our friends, we thought; but the boy's caution was a warning.

There were few Indians in during the afternoon, but under ordinary circumstances we would have thought little of it. As night approached, Ken walked about the store, putting things straight. He put the guns within reach; but even as he did so, he remarked, "What's the use of shooting any of them? We can get as many as we have shells, but they'll get us in the end."

As Ken and I passed each other in the walking about we tried to appear purposeful; we looked at each other as we passed, shrugged, and went on. At dark we were both in the store, with the door wide open and a lamp on either end of the counter. Leaning against the shelves and facing the door, Ken waited. I got pencil and paper and sat down at the counter to write, but I could not sit still, so began putting cookies and peanuts in the bins and setting cans straight on the shelves. When the sound of hoof beats and the squeak of saddle leather reached us, we did not so much as glance at each other. There was whispering in the dark outside, then moccasin feet on the platform and Cla and two disreputable strangers entered. The darkness, we knew, held other men, men who kept themselves beyond the light of the lamps.

Cla stepped forward and put a bit of paper on the counter before Ken. "The stranger rode straight," he said, "not like a man who seeks this way and that and does not know the trail. He looked before and behind and made marks on the paper, as you see. He looked always at the cliffs and the ledges but he made no wrong turnings. The white stranger knew the way to the gold; he made marks on the paper so others would know. He was here; he ate with you, your friend. You are to die before you tell others."

Ken's voice as he answered was low and patient, like some one who has reared a very exasperating child.

"*Deneh*, stand quietly a little while. I would talk to you before you do this thing which you plan. Let those who are outside in the dark with more guns come up near the step, where they can hear my voice.

"Listen to me. You will not have to stay long to hear all I have to say, but first I ask any one of you to step forward here and tell us all of any time when

I have ever lied to any one of you. I wait. Do any
come? No? Then listen again. The man you have
killed was no friend of mine. I tried my best to keep
him from going after the gold. Now he cannot tell
where the gold is; the secret is dead again; it is safe.
I never did know the place; I do not want to know
the place, but I talk too long. You came here to kill
me. May I offer you my own gun to do it with?"

Without any apparently sudden move Ken leaned
forward, took his revolver from under the counter
before him and held it toward Cla, butt first.

For a breath no one moved. The darkness outside was
still too. Cla stepped back uncertainly. Ken waited for
several seconds.

"Here is the gun," he repeated. "Let any one of you
who believes that I lie to you come here and take this
gun. No one? Then you know you are wrong? Let
this night be forgotten then, as if it never had been."

Cla and his two supporters turned and stumbled
through the door; many feet moved from the platform; horses were mounted hastily.

I sat down weakly and listened to the galloping grow
distant. Ken did not move. Suddenly I heard the hoof
beats of one horse running as I had never heard an
Indian horse run. It seemed not to have stopped when
a man leaped on the platform and into the store. It
was Tsay-nez. His face was as white as an Indian's
face could be and his hand was on his gun.

He and Ken looked at each other and all the tense-
ness went out of the Navajo's muscles. "You are safe,
my brother," he said calmly. "I heard, when it might

have been too late, what those who are fools and rascals would do. I came quickly."

"I might have had great need of a friend, but it was Cla and those like him who came."

Both men laughed and Ken told what had happened. When Ken came to the gun incident, Tsay-nez drew his own gun, balanced it on a finger, presented it to Ken butt first and then so quickly I saw only the end of the movement, whirled it about, so that he held the butt and Ken faced the most deadly Indian gun on the reservation. "So, you would have shot Cla, eh, my brother?"

Ken nodded. Again both men laughed and Ken reached for a can of tomatoes. "Cla did not want to be the first to die," Tsay-nez said, as he took the first spoonful. "There were six shots in your gun, six dead men, eh, my brother? And Cla did not bring those with him who would be the six."

Tsay-nez ate and laughed and went away. Days and nights passed, and not by look or word were we reminded of the strange prospector. The Indians came and traded, laughed and wheedled, but never in my life did I have so little desire to own a gold mine.

XVI · WE HEAR MORE OF THE WORLD WAR

ANYTHING in the way of normal Navajo life was welcome. I was even glad to see Old Crazy when he drove his herd of goats past the store in the morning. We could smell him coming and a newer and stronger wave of odor followed him into the open door.

He always shouted at the top of his voice, as if he were calling to some of his flock on a distant hill. *"Ya-de-la-hai-i-i sekiss hai-ya-ha.* Now I am tired, I am hot; I am old and lame. My feet hurt; the sand and the stones hurt my feet because there are holes in my not new moccasins. I need water. Bring me water. Give me some sweet crackers to eat while I drink. No, no. Give me the drink in bottles. I do not want that water in the pail. I can get that kind at the well and colder too. Give me the pink water in the bottle and a white cup to pour it in. What is the good of drinking pink water from a dark bottle? How do I know it is pink? Give me a cup, a white cup, not a tin one or a gray one either. Fifteen cents? Who said anything about fifteen cents? I am thirsty; I have no money. *Ya-de-la,* my grandmother, my throat is aching for drink — pink drink. Hurry up with those sweet crackers while I make a cigarette here. *Ayai-i,* where's all the tobacco gone from this stone bowl? Before you go for the pink water, hand me tobacco and matches."

All this while the smells of forty billy goats pervaded the house and the other Navajos grinned and watched me. One stood behind Old Crazy and motioned that I should comb his hair for him as wives often did for their husbands. Old Crazy's hair always looked as if it had never been combed; it stood in matted straggling points in all directions. This and his wild and insane eye suggested to us his name, and it was not until long after that we learned the Indians too called him Crazy. What his real name was we never knew.

The rest liked to tease me about him and tell me that I should comb his hair and clean him up, so that he would not smell so bad of goats. The old fellow did not come often and I knew he really was hungry most of the time, so I always gave him something to eat, but I never could enjoy doing it when he ordered me about so and smelled up the house; but, as Ken said, "Feed him quickly and let him get away." He always left smacking his lips and with all the tobacco from the stone bowl wrapped up in a little dirty rag he had torn out of his sleeve. His goats were waiting outside for him and we heard them all bleating together, as the atmosphere cleared about the store and the Indians laughingly told me to make a new shirt for him.

In some ways we felt shut far away from the war, closer to the Arizona sunsets. Ken was over age, but I was not and wondered what I could do.

Our only real touch with what the whole world was concentrating on was through the wholesalers. In every mail and by special messengers we received such notes as, "Send all the cowhides you can get. Pay twice the usual price. The government is letting contracts for army shoes, harness, etc." Again it was, "Send all the horsehair you can. Pay fifty cents for a tail. Manufacturers demand curled horsehair."

The 1917 wool season was an all-time high in quantity of wool demanded and in prices. The Indians had more money than ever before; forty cents a pound for wool was unique to them.

As stock-buying season approached, traders were telling them that lambs and sheep would be worth much money and that they should sell all they could because never would white men pay as much again. Ken did not approve of this and rode every day to some distant hogan where the Indians had big flocks to tell them that they must not sell too close, that in a few years they would have no flocks, if they sold too many now.

The big stockmen came in to talk over selling and Ken explained that they must keep all female stock except the very old, and that these must all be sold first, at the highest price they would bring. Next should be sold all of the steers over two years old and all the wethers over one year. He rode through each Indian herd and marked the male animals that should be kept. All others might go to the corrals for sale.

Of course, all of the Indians did not hold by this advice, but the wisest of them did; and more came to see that Ken was right. He told them that he would buy this way and that none of them should bring to our corral any but the animals that he told them they should sell. There were weeks and weeks of riding up and down the country before the buying season opened, so most of the trading fell to me.

Teddy-Witte became veteran cow horses and took turns on the rides, so I always had one in the corral for company and to tell me when Ken was coming over the hill.

In our early days on the reservation I was always being surprised at something the poor benighted heathen did. Though Ken spoke of the Indians as heathen, it was a friendly, even a complimentary term, and he often warned me that they were neither heathen nor benighted.

As the months passed, I learned to respect the way the Navajos made the most of an arid, rocky land; I admired their architecture; the design of the blankets and the skill and sincerity in carrying it out were real art. As a rule they were industrious; the lazy and the indigent were less common than among whites. Their religion was wholesome and clean and their respect for their belief compared favorably with the white man's attitude toward his God. I could not enough admire the sand paintings.

In the fall of 1917 I heard more of the Navajo singing than we usually heard.

Whenever a "sing" or ceremony of any kind was approaching, we heard much vocal practice. A group of older men and young ones sat on the ground in the shade of the store and sang. When any one made a mistake, the older man leading stopped, sang the passage alone, as he beat the time; and they all tried again — and perhaps again and again and many times more. This continued for hours.

Sometimes a group gathered in our camp hogan and had an all-night rehearsal. A Navajo voice is the only sound I have ever heard which could, on a low note, fill my ears with a deep, powerful vibrating that was both feeling and sound. Often I went to sleep with this pulsating sound from the hogan fairly filling the whole valley. After hours of sleep I woke perplexed and uneasy at the vibration before I was awake enough to recognize the sound.

Often the men sang as they rode and we heard their voices long before we saw them. They seemed to keep time to the ponies' gait, no matter what the gait might be. Occasionally four or five men rode in, pulled their ponies to a halt, dismounted, tied the horses and came toward the store still singing, still in perfect unison and without a break for breath or to allow for exercise or changing positions.

One day something far more remarkable happened.

MORE OF THE WORLD WAR

Half a dozen Indians and I were in the store. The trading was done, but my callers were resting, visiting and waiting to ride home in the delicious coolness that follows the setting of the sun. The door was open. A faint, sweet, far-away note floated in and then a quaver like nothing I had ever heard before. I listened and looked toward Clizzy do-clizzy Begay (Blue Goat's son).

"Who sings?" I asked.

We all listened. Then, prompted by a unanimous, silent urge, we moved to the platform outside the door. The sun was down; there wasn't a movement anywhere; the air was clear and soft and blue. No one was in sight; but the distant voice filled the whole valley with the sweetest, smoothest notes I have ever heard. They seemed not so loud as they seemed power-ful, but any voice that carried so in the open must have volume back of it.

The Indians looked knowingly from one to another and nodded as they looked. "The Singer," one said. "The Singer as we heard him thirty years ago."

Now I could distinguish the sound of a horse gallop-ing on a hard trail, and then over a hill and through the piñons came a pony and rider. Swinging his quirt, his head thrown back, he poured out the most beautiful, wild, paganish sounds. I can't begin to describe them. Straight toward us he galloped and, pulling his horse to a sliding stop directly in front of the platform, he sat swaying in his saddle until he finished his song. His audience never stirred.

When the song was ended, there was that second of

silence that is more appreciative than any applause;
and then the Indians seized upon and greeted their
old friend. Bursting with curiosity, I went behind the
counter to get him something to eat. How could any
old, wrinkled man make such wonderful sounds as we
had heard? And how was it that in the months when
he had been bringing a goathide or a small bundle of
wool to the store, I had not learned of his talent? To
be sure the Indians called him the Singer, but I had
not realized that the name fitted this common-looking
old fellow. All Navajo men were singers and good ones
too, so far as I could discover; but this man's voice
was superior to any that I had ever heard, white or
Indian.

Now the Singer, humming between swallows, leaned
heavily on the counter as he ate crackers and canned
tomatoes. Clizzy do-clizzy Begay called for a spoon
and took his turn dipping into the can. None of the
others offered to do this, but they all talked and
laughed together of the days when this grand voice
led the sings and of the coming sing at To-Clazin's
hogan.

I did not have the language to tell how much I
thought of the singing; but I did my best, and the
Singer, his kindly face a map of merry lines, understood. "*A-la-honi*," he grinned, "to-day I am a young
man again and I sing with myself all across the valley
from Saluni. The white trader at that place gave me
a drink of red wine, — wine not like any I ever tasted
before. It was dark and soft as black lamb's wool.
We drank together; and, as I came past the white

rocks where the antelope used to play, my youth returned to me. The old songs came back and I remembered that I was the Singer. Hear me now as I ride home. I'll sing you the song of the trails as I sang it thirty years ago. *A-la-honi,* my children, to-day I am young again."

In another moment he was gone and the trail song of the Navajo came back to us in delicate waves of sound that were gorgeous as a rainbow. I wanted to cry.

When the sound had melted into the distance, the after-sunset light had become blue, dark and starry. The other Indians, with cigarettes made of corn husk and our tobacco, stood on the platform discussing the Singer. Evidently for years he had been so much better than the others, he had been unanimously named; now he was old and did not sing unless he had a drink. They commented on why the drink made him sing and agreed that whatever the Englishman gave him worked better than the white man's whisky they gave him last time.

Why do we try to thrust our civilization on a people like this?

Ladies' Night

A dance is a serial affair, in a different place each night. The crowd gathered at Covered Water about noon. There were wagons and yellow-geared top buggies, but mostly ponies — dozens of them. The families camped, put up brush shelters and borrowed tubs of me to cook the freshly killed sheep and goats, and we soon had the house covered with pelts for the first time since winter. Ken and I joined them in the yard and ate roast ribs that were turned on a stick over an open fire and bread fried in tallow. Our friends were very cordial and enjoyed our eating with them.

By night the little store was jammed to overflowing. It seemed that every one had to buy a white shirt, or a silk 'kerchief for head bandie, or oranges, or soda pop. I stayed to look on, but Ken went to bed after the trading was over.

This was called the women's dance; the girls dragged the men out to dance unless the men paid promptly and escaped. I watched one girl pulling at a boy, but he had both arms wound about the spokes of a wagon wheel and she had to give him up. Another was pulling mightily when the man suddenly followed her. She went sprawling, but she took the man with her and when they got to their feet she still had hold of his shirt.

White Hat came along in a new brown suit and dared me to dance. The step seemed simple, so I took him out. How they did roar and laugh when I trotted backwards around him! Then I forgot to collect! The women have to be paid for each dance. Anything from ten cents up to fifty.

I did not stay up all night and try to sleep under the wagon this time, but came home and went properly to bed. The next morning Ken told me to take a lot of calico, candy and oranges up to some of the head men. I went loaded down. All the riders were sitting on their horses around the new green-covered hogan that had been erected for the occasion. The oldest medicine man lodged there. The singers were standing in front, facing the door. I gave my load to Hosteen Dugien Begay, who took it inside.

In a minute he came out and began throwing the candy in handfuls over the singers. They grabbed and caught it as it fell around them, but never stopped singing. The oranges followed the candy and some one in the crowd called out for some. Dugi threw them as far as he could and those on horseback scrambled for them. Suddenly from the smoke hole in the top of the hogan came the bundles of calico, each bundle tied in a hard knot, so it would throw easily. You can believe the singers caught the pieces. Next out of the hogan came the girls who had danced. Some had rolls of calico, one had a buckskin, and some had new robes. They walked into the crowd and gave the bundles to the men of their choice. Finally a headman came out with a roll of calico and a robe and gave it to the drummer, who had never missed a beat and so could not scramble with the rest.

That was the end. I watched the crowd string out across the mesa. There were all colors of ponies with riders in all colors of shirts, head bands and handkerchiefs, silver belts and buttons, coral, white shell and turquoise beads.

Indian Draft

Our quiet life was disturbed again and again by the mail sack as Hosteen Sendol-zhi brought the roll of rotogravure sheets which Mother sent us from the

New York Times. These brought the war nearer to us than anything else, unless it was the food question, but the food in a beef and mutton-eating country was not so much of a problem.

We had never used our quota of sugar, so we did not have to cut down there. We liked coarse breads. Our only real problem was selling the Indians corn meal. In fact, we couldn't reason them away. Why and grinding was better than what we had to sell, so it was hard to reason away their arguments that they should be allowed to buy flour without buying corn meal. In fact, we couldn't reason them away. Why should they buy what they had no use for? One man flatly refused to carry the meal home, after he had paid for it. He said the children mixed it with the sand to play with, and when it rained, the meal made a messy dooryard of what was usually nice clean sand.

To return to the pictures. The brown sheet showed photographs of the crowds in Paris, the streets jammed, soldiers marching, flags everywhere.

The page was always immediately spread out on the counter, and as many Indians as could get near crowded around and looked and asked questions. They pointed and marveled. I marveled, too, at the real intelligence with which they studied the picture. Not one of them had ever been farther from the reservation than the railroad towns a hundred miles to the south and east, but of course they recognized the buildings. They counted the stories and the windows and guessed that a particular building would be as high as such and such a rock or bluff. They recognized cars and automobiles and identified soldiers by the uniforms, and they counted all of them.

One day, when they despaired of counting so many people as there were in the picture of massed crowds, one took a soda-pop bottle, borrowed my pencil, and drew circles all over the sheet. Then they counted the people in each circle and asked me to add the numbers. After that they estimated that there were four persons in each space not included in the circles and I added those numbers. It came to several thousand and they repeated the figure all day, trying to grasp the magnitude of it in people. They speculated on how many sheep and horses all the Navajos owned, and the number of people was greater than the number of animals. At last they decided the stars were the only thing as numerous, or maybe the grass.

Looking at a picture of a battleship with a close-up of the guns, they were quite "floored" when I told them the guns would shoot thirty miles, about a day's ride, and blow a great hole in the ground besides. That wouldn't quite go down and they called Ken and asked him.

The army planes in a picture were flying in a formation like a flock of wild geese. The Indians asked if they would come down at water holes. They couldn't get away from the idea that things that flew had bird habits even if men did ride in them.

In a few days the brown sheets would be worn to rags; every inch had been pawed over and discussed. Always questions followed: How many white people left? Pretty soon, maybe so, Navajos will be the only people left. When all the white men are dead, what will the white women do?

Calico went up in price from ten and twelve cents a yard to twenty and twenty-five cents. That was tragedy, but more tragic was the fact that a velvet shirt that had cost $1.50 now cost $3.50.

The Little Wind Doctor raved because there was no more free tobacco in the bowl on our counter. We explained that the soldiers had to have the cigarettes. That did not convince the old fellow that he should not have any. I told him that the small sack of tobacco with the bull on it would cost just twice what it had after our stock on hand was gone. Perhaps we would not be able to get any more at any price. In our last loads of freight had been some bags of a different kind of tobacco — I think it must have been intended for pipes. I filled the bowl with that, but the old man wailed and raved. He said it was no good and his granddaughter, meaning me, was so cruel that she wouldn't let an old man who was her ancestor have real tobacco. To quiet the old man, we gave him some of our small stock of the old tobacco, and he went off muttering.

He couldn't see why all the fuss. He had been hearing for many days that many white men were being killed every day. There were not enough left so they needed all the tobacco.

Another old Indian wanted the barbed wire when the war was done. He would use it to fence his desert water hole. He looked at the pictures and said they didn't seem to know how to make a good fence over there, so he would take enough to surround a bit of grass for pasture; they seemed to have so much tangled up and going to waste.

A picture of a long line of ambulances and hospital interiors impressed all the Indians. One asked if their mothers knew when the soldiers were hurt and who would, and how could they bury the dead where there were no quiet out-of-sight places.

One studied the pictures for a long time and said soberly, "*Dechi do hiyia a-sun al-so de-chi*," meaning, "Much weeping. All the women will cry."

They seemed to get as much of a story from the pictures as one might from reading.

And then suddenly the Navajos ceased to think how other men fought and began to plan their own campaigns.

The news that every Navajo man must go to Fort Defiance to register started the unrest; and then, when all about us was a constant boiling of questions and uneasiness, some unwise and short-sighted trader started the tale that the registered Indians were to be compelled to go to war and would be put in the front and shot first to save the white men.

Our Indians admitted they must go to the fort; they agreed they would do anything Washington said but — and here Navajos like Little Bidoni and Tsay-Nez looked straight at each other — "We will not leave our own homes and country." No one watching them could doubt the finality of that.

For days the trading was slack; several came to sit out in the camp hogan and powwow. They were be-

ginning to doubt that the white men were the friends
they were pretending to be. I noticed two Indians
carrying guns. Perhaps any other time I would not
have seen that as they all had guns and often carried
them. Then one morning a strange Indian came into
the store and bought every rifle cartridge we had for
the 30-30 carbines, the most used gun with them.
Ken said I should not have sold him the cartridges;
but the Indian could see we had them and because
I did not want him to know I was afraid to sell them
to him, I asked if the coyotes were getting his sheep
and he said yes.

Some of the Indians had the old Springfield muskets,
rare old guns that would look well in a museum.

Ken said he thought the old men would keep the
young hotheads quiet. Thinking they had better be
where we could feed them than to get excited on an
empty stomach and do something rash, he encouraged
them to meet at the post any time and talk things
over among themselves.

Another two weeks went by and all the men of
fighting age had been registered. Every day the talk
went on. The plan was this: When the first sign of an
order came for the Indians to leave the reservation,
those around each store were to kill the trader and
his family and burn the store. The pawn was to be
saved and returned to the owners and the supplies
saved, if possible, for the Indians' use. They would all
rise and act on the same day. When the stores were
burned, and we noted that they figured that they
could use clubs at the stores and save their ammunition,

they would all march on the railroad towns and fire and kill as long as they were able. The white soldiers and guns were all across the sea, so the Indians reasoned they might destroy many towns before any one could stop them.

In the days that followed, I fed our visitors often on coffee and doughnuts or crackers and canned tomatoes but they went without a song — just whipped their ponies over the hills and out of sight. Ken and I looked at each other and said nothing.

After many a day when we had heard plenty of desperate plans, the moon came up soft and white; every rock and piñon stood out black and clear; everything was still — the sort of stillness that made us feel how very far we were from — any one.

How like paradise the ranch would be! No one could say we hadn't earned it. If we were left alive to get to it, I never wanted to see, hear or smell an Indian again.

I was tired! Tired!

Some Indians coming from Chin Lee brought the news that traders there were sending their women folk out to distant homes or relatives; only men were seen about the different posts. Even Tsay-nez asked if I would go soon and when I told him no, that I liked it and would stay there, he looked queerly at me and went off to talk to Ken.

A special messenger came in from Fort Defiance with a letter from the Indian agent in charge. Ken smiled grimly as he read it. "Dear Sir: We have before us a request from Mr. R. J. Sidney at the Saluni post east of your store, stating that there is immediate danger of an Indian uprising and urging us to send military protection to his place. Before we request Washington to take so extreme a measure, Mr. Taylor of Lugontale has advised that we ask you to send in a report of Indian conditions that may be causing concern to Mr. Sidney."

The day this letter came and before we could reply, Ken listened, by invitation, to the big Navajo powwow held at the post. About a hundred and twenty-five Indians sat on the shady slope by the camp hogan, ate doughnuts and coffee, and smoked cigarettes and then one, and another, and another talked. They kept it up all day. For the first time I realized where the Indians got their name of being serious and unsmiling. The sun went down and the moon, what there was of it, came up, and still they talked. I was tired out and ready to drop. About midnight I went to bed and tried to sleep.

I think I had dozed off when the most blood-curdling uproar brought me to my feet in the middle of the floor. Horses were clattering over the trail, quirts were slashing and saddles squeaking. At last I distinguished Ken's voice in the farewells and I let my breath out.

Next the Navajos' riding song floated through the night. We hadn't heard that for weeks — not since the men went to the fort to be registered — and how beautiful, how perfectly uplifting it sounded.

I was almost in tears before Ken could tell me what had happened. After he had told me, I could not decide whether to weep for joy or apprehension, so I did

292

neither, but went to sleep and slept all night, or what was left of it.

It was just like Ken to think of the solution that would suit the would-be-warriors but might not please other white men.

Ken reported that first one and then another talked. The young men were for organizing a massacre and killing as many whites as they could before soldiers could be brought in. Some eighteen thousand fighting men had registered and they had bought all the ammunition on the reservation. Killing the whites on the reservations would have been no job at all; they would scarcely be in good training by the time they reached the towns. They knew all that only too well.

The older ones could remember Kit Carson and his scouts and they did not want trouble. The young fellows answered with the story that the Indians were to be sent across the sea, put in the front lines and killed first.

Toward midnight they asked Ken to talk, and with nothing but his own conviction to go on, he made several serious promises.

At one time the Mexicans had owned the Black Mountain country; quarrels over land were within the memory of all Navajos and within the experience of many.

Ken told his audience that if the Indians were called to fight, it would be to protect their own hogans, their own families and their own wide valleys from the Mexicans. He told them that if they were called for that purpose, Washington would see to it that they were made soldiers and provided with all they needed. He told them that if they were called off the reservation, he would go with them and lead them.

It was what they wanted to believe and they believed it.

The morning after the conference, we sent a special messenger with a letter to the agent but felt none too comfortable while we waited four days for the answer. When it came, it was hearty approval of what Ken had done.

We knew that Ken had probably averted a massacre, but at best the situation that followed was a doubtful joke. Ken might have to make good on some of his promises.

The Indians were getting their herds in shape as any white man would if he expected to leave home; saying moccasins would not do for long marches, they bought heavy shoes. Old men and all wanted to start south to meet the Mexicans.

We had to do everything we could to hold them down. So sure were they that what Ken had said would happen, that they spread the news everywhere. If some one in authority had contradicted Ken's statements, we would not long have been making speeches about war policy or anything else.

However, for a time all was friendly and beautiful. The traders who had sent their families out brought them back and laughed at their foolish fears. They thought they knew all the time what would happen.

Na-ho-hi, the Glorious Fourth, was held at the store twenty-five miles from us, so we had a quiet day. A few women and children came in and visited me. I had to feed them, of course, and they went away happy.

They talked about when "our men" should go to kill the Mexicans and asked if I would stay and keep the store while Ken was gone. I said I would. Wild promises seemed to be the thing!

As I checked out another four-horse load of beef and horsehides, I commented to Ken that I believed I was the only woman in the allied countries who was not knitting, and I didn't so much as own a needle. It was a real comfort when Ken said that perhaps it would count for something that I handled so much of the wool before it was made into yarn.

Autumn was coming. Still no call to start for the border. Some one asked every day and I began to think Ken was as anxious to go as the Indians. We did not hear that any Mexican was attacked, but the Mexican teamsters did not come on to the reservation; they did not feel comfortable there. The Indians did all the freight hauling.

I was pleased when To-Clazhin brought me some sewing to do. I made him a red velvet vest with five pockets, buttonholes for six silver buttons and a real buckle at the back. For weeks they had not thought of sewing.

Now my customers were coming back, and I took the vest into the store and worked on it; it was good for them to see home interest again and forget their guns.

XVII · QUICK DEATH

AND suddenly, from the skies there fell the most trying and saddest experience we lived through on the reservation.

It had been a piñon-nut year. The nut-bearing section was from five to ten miles from our post.

The wholesalers sent out word that piñon nuts would be seven cents a pound, so we ordered sacks for shipping and told our Indians to bring in all they could.

The frost opened the cones, but the Indians did not wait for the nuts to fall; they knocked them from the tree with sticks and picked them up one by one from the ground. Women and children did the work. They left their comfortable hogans just at the season when frost was getting nippy and went in wagonloads to the trees.

296

QUICK DEATH

While dozens of families were scattered over forty square miles of piñon woods in open camps, the cold fall rains began; and the influenza hit those people.

The first news we had was brought by White Hat's oldest son. Two other trading posts were nearer than ours to the woods, but he came to us. Since he had ridden without a blanket, he was wet through and draggled; but there was a kind of dignity in the way he told of his mother's death and of the other children lying sick under the trees in the rain.

Like a grass fire the disease swept the Indian country. Every day some one told of deaths. The exhausted medicine men seemed to rest only when they stopped at the store to be warmed and fed, while they told of treatments and deaths. Before we had recovered from the first shock, the Old Buzzard was gone; three of the Old Lady's grandchildren and one of our best teamsters died the first week. The survivors who came to the store were thin and weak and pathetic. They asked for medicine, the strong medicine in the arm we had used for smallpox, or anything. It was help they wanted and we could do nothing.

A dwelling where a death occurred was always vacated immediately; for miles around every good winter hogan was deserted. The living moved out into the rain and found what shelter they could in temporary camps. Here death came again and those who were left moved on.

At first, leaving Ken at the store, I rode to the hogans to help where I could. It was truly terrible. Where one day I saw ponies in the corral, children in the dooryard, and warm smoke curling from the roof of a hogan, the next day there would be no vestige of daily living; but instead the cold rain falling on an absolutely deserted home or an overturned pan or basket placed before the door of a hogan, empty save for an unburied body.

With one exception, it was only when the dead outnumbered the living in a family that a body was left unburied. In this one instance the dead man was Hosteen Cla's old father, husband of the Old Buzzard, a withered, disreputable old fellow who lived alone and cared for the buck herd. Ken, riding past his hogan, heard his two scrawny dogs howling and on riding closer saw that they were starving. He looked in; then rode to Hosteen Cla and told him the old man was dead.

Cla and his brothers were too lazy, afraid, or possibly too sick to go care for the body. Anyhow, no one went. Those people never liked to go near one who has died alone; but, under the circumstances, we thoroughly despised Cla's household and gave our strength and attention elsewhere. Still they did nothing.

In a few days Cla came to ask why Ken did not go bury the old man. Ken replied that we were doing all we could for families that had no strong men like himself and his brothers left and insisted that Cla go look after his father's body.

Cla refused and asked that we write a letter to the priest at Chin Lee and have him come do it. I agreed to do this if Cla would go for the Father with a team and buggy and take him home afterwards. Cla was

298

satisfied; but the next day, when we thought he was well on his way to Chin Lee, he reappeared to say that it was too far and too cold; he did not care to drive to Chin Lee.

Ken could stand no more. He didn't say anything to Cla but motioned him to get on his horse. Cla hesitated a second and then, though Ken had still not spoken, he backed out of the store and scrambled onto his horse where he sat in the rain, waiting.

He didn't have long to wait. Ken kept one of our horses saddled all the time. I asked him why he was carrying a gun. He did not stop but answered as he went out of the door, "Not for that skunk."

Ken shot the two dogs, which were almost dead from starvation, and then forced Cla to help burn the hogan over the old man's body.

One day a woman came into the store, put her head on my shoulder and cried quietly. After a little she asked for a box in which to bury her little boy. There were two others dead in her hogan she told me, but she could not move them. The little boy she could lift, so she came for clothes and a box to use for a coffin.

I asked her why she wanted a box when *deneh* never used boxes to bury their dead, and this was her reason: An older son who had gone to the white man's school at Riverside, many miles by the steam train away, had told her that it was a good way, used by the white people when they buried the Navajo or other school children who died at the school, and no buildings had to be burned down or deserted. He had not noticed any ill luck had followed such burials, therefore he thought it was perhaps the box that kept the gods from being angry because the buildings were not burned.

Now times were so distressing that anything that had ever pleased the gods might well be tried; maybe they wanted boxes; maybe it would help to have a coffin; gods should be propitiated when *deneh* died by dozens. What did I think, and did I have a box that the gods might approve of?

I said perhaps she was right; we should try everything that might help. Together she and I went through our pile of empty boxes. Carefully saving every nail, we knocked a coffee case to pieces. She tied the boards to her saddle and borrowed the hammer to nail them together again at home. I begged her to return the hammer, but she never did. It had to be left at the grave.

It was that evening that Ken came home from a long ride and went directly to the bed and lay down. For three days he lay with his face to the wall and would not speak. I did for him everything I knew; but there was so little, so terribly little to do.

Twice a day I locked him in, while I watered and fed the horses. I dared not let the Indians know how sick he was nor did I dare let them care for Teddy-Witte, lest I never see the horses again. Will I ever forget those three days? Never had we seemed so far from any one, so terribly alone.

Ken was not unconscious, but the only way he knew to be sick was an animal's way — to crawl off alone and wait. On the fourth day he spoke and I knew he was better. He was unbelievably weak and for days gained very slowly. No one will ever know the relief I felt when the Indians could see him about once more.

After a month, deaths were less frequent and we hoped the worst was over. Ken seemed almost himself. There was even some cattle buying. But no one was out of the shadow of what we had all been through.

One day Hosteen Tso came in. I had not seen him since before the epidemic and the man was so thin his clothes hung on him. He leaned against the counter.

"You have been very sick, my friend," I said.

With that he told me that his family of ten was the only family he knew of where not one was missing. They even had one more, a little two-year-old girl he had found crying in Hosteen Be-Dugi-Clazhin's hogan, where all the other members of the family lay dead about the cold ashes.

"No, I was not sick," he said. "In those first days when the rains were cold and the *deneh* were sick and died everywhere, two of my boys had the very hot bodies and could not get up. I went for a medicine man, and another, and another, many of them, but they were sick themselves or were singing the chants for others who had the sickness. All of two days I rode but could find no one to go to my hogan to save my boys. At home I found the women and all of the other children, nine altogether, were very, very sick too. The baby who is four was the worst. He asked me to help him. What would you have done, my mother? I rode away again, seeking a medicine man. Where the cedar trees grow thick on the hill that stops suddenly I got off my horse to pray. I prayed to several *deneh* gods

301

that know me; then I knew I must be the doctor for
my family and I took berries from the cedar trees and
gathered plants here and there. It was slow work in
the rain, but there were those nine sick ones in my
hogan.

"The plants and the berries I boiled with water in the
coffeepots and gave each of my family a drink. I sang
one of the songs for healing and gave another a drink.
So I timed the doses until the medicine was gone, and
I rode out and got more plants and made the medicine
and the sick ones drank.

"There were days when no one came to my hogan.
I did not sleep but sang the prayers and gave the medicine until all of my family were well.

"At the last, some *deneh* riding by saw me and asked
me to come to their hogans. I am not a medicine man,
but on the hill of cedar trees I told the gods who know
me about the medicine and the chants; and then I went
to other hogans, many of them. The food was not always good; and I did not sleep much, so I am thin."

"But these people with the sickness, they could not
pay," I said.

Hosteen Tso did not seem to hear. "I am thin," he
repeated, "and I think my horse is glad, no? He is thin
too, so he does not want to carry a heavy man."

"You are wise and good, my father," I said, feeling
heartily ashamed that I had done so little. "You will
now be a big medicine man and earn many cattle with
your healing."

"No, no, my grandmother. It was only for this time
and because my prayer was right for me and the need

great that the gods helped, but no more. I am no doctor."

October was cattle-buying season, but all that business was so lacking in activity it seemed somehow uncanny and unnatural. Ken wanted to buy and the Indians wanted to sell; but until the very last of the month Ken was not able to ride much to see the stock and the Navajos could not bring the animals in.

Never did Ken's remarkable memory serve him better. A Navajo would say, "I will sell you a four-year-old steer. He is red with white spots and is worth forty dollars."

And Ken would answer, "All right, but bring me the one with the short horns that curve, so, and the white spot that is so and so on the left side. I will not pay forty dollars for any other steer in your herd."

He bought animals from herds he had not seen for months and the Indians brought the purchased stock faithfully.

Many of the deals were interrupted or closed with farewells. It was in November, 1914, that we had gone to Covered Water, and now in November, 1918, we were planning to leave. The cattle money would mean that we had paid enough on the farm so that we could call it ours, and could now go to it and hope to finish the payments with earnings from the farm itself.

"*Aye-ah-e*," a Navajo would say to Ken. "And so you buy no more steers! And who will buy our wool? Some man we do not like. It is not good." And he would go away, shaking his head.

The Little Bidoni knew of Ken's going, but he did

not mention it either when he sold Ken his steers or when they were delivered. Usually some members of his family brought the cattle in, but this last time he was to see Ken he brought them himself.

"It is done, my friend," he said, when his wagons were loaded with goods and his cattle had been paid for. He and Ken clasped hands, and the little Navajo walked out very straight and without looking back. Ken nodded. To him that was a man's way of acting.

When Tsay-nez did not come in, I mentioned it with surprise, but Ken only said, "He will not come. Why should he?"

I was busy putting dish towels in my ranch hope chest, packing our one cherished piece of ancient pottery and even one of the Old Buzzard's round-bottomed black jars. Ken objected to that but said nothing when I added to the small pile of Indian blankets we were taking the one the Old Lady had left unfinished.

The women clung to me, brought me their children for whom I had made dresses and shirts, or leaned on my shoulder to name with a sob those who had gone.

"How many days — come back?" they asked, and when at last they understood that we were not coming back, "What will you do in the new hogan? It is a store, no? Then what will you do?"

Nazhuni Yazzi came to the store alone and said good-by to Ken as his father had done. When the door closed behind him, Ken turned back to the store and stared with eyes that I knew were, for a moment unseeing, at the shelves of canned goods.

QUICK DEATH

The men joked a little about going to the Mexican border and Ken promised to come back to them if Washington called them to fight.

I had not realized that we had woven so many threads of friendship that it hurt to break them. I stopped often to think that in all my life these four years were the most isolated and the most colorful.

The man who had bought the store arrived and took control. We were relieved to be able to give our whole time to packing and getting away.

The old camp outfit with which we had come from the coast was to take us from Covered Water over Cottonwood Pass to the farm.

On the morning of November 13, we sat in the wagon headed for the pass and thinking of the four days of hard going before we reached it, when a messenger rode up with the news of the Armistice.

For a little we said nothing. Ken released the brake, let the reins go loose on the horses' backs and turned to me.

"Now you won't have to learn to knit," he grinned.

P134 Indians called "Leathers"